Why You Shouldn't Kill Yourself

Why You Shouldn't Kill Yourself

Five Tricks of the Heart about Assisted Suicide

SUSAN WINDLEY-DAOUST

CASCADE *Books* · Eugene, Oregon

WHY YOU SHOULDN'T KILL YOURSELF
Five Tricks of the Heart about Assisted Suicide

Cascade Books
An Imprint of Wipf and Stock Publishers
199 W. 8th Ave., Suite 3
Eugene, OR 97401

www.wipfandstock.com

PAPERBACK ISBN: 978-1-4982-9143-9
HARDCOVER ISBN: 978-1-4982-9145-3
EBOOK ISBN: 978-1-4982-9144-6

Cataloguing-in-Publication data:

Names: Windley-Daoust, Susan.

Title: Why you shouldn't kill yourself : five tricks of the heart about assisted suicide / Susan Windley-Daoust.

Description: Eugene, OR: Cascade Books, 2018 | Includes bibliographical references and index.

Identifiers: ISBN 978-1-4982-9143-9 (paperback) | ISBN 978-1-4982-9145-3 (hardcover) | ISBN 978-1-4982-9144-6 (ebook)

Subjects: LCSH: Theological anthropology. | Assisted suicide. | Title.

Classification: BJ1533.H9 K37 2018 (paperback) | BJ1533 (ebook)

Manufactured in the U.S.A.   03/15/18

Dedicated to my father, Curtis Jackson Windley
1929–2016

The heart is devious above all else; it is perverse—
who can understand it?

—Jer 17:9

The heart is the dwelling-place where I am, where I live; according
to the Semitic or Biblical expression, the heart is the place "to which
I withdraw." The heart is our hidden center, beyond the grasp of our
reason and of others; only the Spirit of God can fathom the human
heart and know it fully. *The heart is the place of decision, deeper than
our psychic drives. It is the place of truth, where we choose life or death.* It
is the place of encounter, because as image of God we live in relation: it
is the place of covenant.

—*Catechism of the Catholic Church* § 2563 (italics added)

...You shall not stand by idly when your neighbor's life is at stake.

—Lev 19:16 (NAB)

Contents

Permissions

Acknowledgments

I am deeply grateful to a variety of people who served as readers to part or all of this project: Fr. Andrew Beerman, Fr. Andrew Dickinson, Allen Hickerson, Ryan Langr, Lorelle Pysh, Jaye Procure, Alison Rose, and Fr. David Smith. I am also indebted to others for medically oriented conversations on this topic, specifically, Wes Ely, MD; Natalie Rodden, MD; Annmarie Hosie, PhD; and Donna Kamann, CNP. Finally, I thank Eileen Schaller and two anonymous donors for covering permissions costs incurred on the way to publication.

Any mistakes or misjudgments are entirely my own.

Preface to Theologians and Pastors

Nothing would seem more common, more inflexible, more historically stable than the experience of death—our own deaths, or the death of a loved one. And yet, how we perceive and approach death has changed dramatically (both medically and culturally) in the past few decades. The culmination of these changes is found in increasing public support for physician-assisted suicide. This book tries to present the challenge of physician-assisted suicide as a misguided contemporary quest for "safe passage."

Phillippe Ariès (1914–1984), a historian of family and daily life, argues that in centuries past human beings died "a tame death." That is, dying was a known process that was expected and folded into the realities of everyday life. People died at home, of course, because there were few hospitals. Medical care was largely palliative care, focused on keeping the person comfortable. The person dying was usually in the center of known ways of family life until the very end . . . a bed brought into a living area, for example, and receiving visitors: family, friends, doctors, a priest. Although dying could be physically and emotionally difficult, there was a reassuring sense of place in it. Death, indeed, was part of life, along with birth, love, grief, joy, pleasure, and sadness.[1]

1. Phillippe Ariès' work is referenced substantially in Daniel Callahan's

But with the rise of modern medicine, Ariès says our perspective on the place of death has tilted. Now, we perceive death as inherently wild, and something that we need to domesticate through medical care. The "wild death" is marked by an uncertainty throughout the experience of dying: at the hospital or at home? Will this cure work, or not? How long should I fight? This looks like the end—but wait, we have other options. Time in an ICU, away from most family and friends, and surrounded by beeping monitors, is likely. Aries argues that modern medicine's quest to cure—in itself a good thing—does unfortunately result in a kind of "technological brinkmanship" that results in people actively fighting the disease or injury up to hours before they actually die. People dying never leave fight mode.

Because doctors and patients never leave fight mode, a lack of cure is a perceived, by some, as a failure . . . as if death is not our common end.

Great work has been accomplished in the hospice movement—a movement that has called for people to have a relatively comfortable experience of dying, ideally at home, with pain issues addressed, and family or friends around. But most people, at this point, do not know how to be around someone who is dying. We don't know how to die at home. The only dying ritual we know is the one defined by fighting and control. Hospice is quite the counterculture to many, and those who find themselves facing the dying process may not see why anyone would *not* choose to fight for control.

The contemporary experience of dying, the "wild death," has become, more and more, a human quest for safe passage. But most people translate that understandable quest into a desire for absolute control. They see that the only way to not hurt, to avoid pain, is to maintain control. And physician-assisted suicide is the most intense formula of maintaining absolute control.

---

popular book *The Troubled Dream of Life: In Search of a Peaceful Death*, 26–27. Ariès's most relevant work, *The Hour of Our Death*, is a magnum opus on how Europeans experienced death from the Greco–Roman era to the nineteenth century.

Less a moral treatise, more written to the spiritually lost

As you can surmise, my approach to this topic is not, in the first place, moral. I do think assisted suicide is gravely wrong, and certainly moral questions are addressed in this text. (Although physician-assisted suicide opens a whole host of moral side issues that I do not touch on much at all: conscience protections for doctors, nurses, and hospices, the voice of family members in decision-making, the influence of money—or lack of it—in decision-making, the rights of people living with disabilities, and so forth. But these are being addressed in many venues.[2] People know suicide is wrong. It takes a lot of mental effort to intentionally end one's own life: healthy people act to preserve their lives. We actively try to prevent suicide in any other case. The reason increasing numbers of people find physician-assisted suicide attractive is that people are spiritually lost.

I do not mean that in any accusatory manner. I mean that people have actively chosen not to have a spiritual home, and we know this through the increasing number of surveys that indicate a sharply rising increase in the "nones"—the segment of the population that does not identify with a religion. Sometimes they self-identify as "spiritual, not religious." Sometimes they bear this bumper sticker on their cars: "all who wander are not lost." I will be candid: many religions in the United States bear responsibility for this. I can understand why people could say they believe in God, but not fully trust religious institutions. We've made trust harder than it should be.

But . . . this move to "spiritual, not religious" is clearly not *all* about institutional trustworthiness.[3] I know quite a few of these people—you do, too—and often they say that their limited experience with a religious home was fine. Just not essential, and couldn't

2. An extremely useful compendium of research worldwide regarding assisted suicide and euthanasia can be found in Jones, "Assisted Suicide and Euthanasia."

3. Lipka, "Why America's 'Nones' Left Religion Behind," *Fact Tank: News in the Numbers* (blog), The Pew Research Center.

compete against the allure of the open road, the freedom of wandering and finding your own way. We are a country of self-made men and women—or we like to think so—and that is increasingly including our own religion.

So what's wrong with that? Well, let's begin with dying, and begin with a story. One of the most poignant books I have ever read is a memoir titled *My Own Country* by Abraham Verghese,[4] an Indian-American infectious diseases doctor working in the mountains of East Tennessee during the beginning of the AIDS epidemic. The book is about how medical doctors came to learn to diagnose and treat that disease when all was mystery and fear—but even more so, the book is about home. Verghese began noticing that all these initial AIDS patients—mostly homosexual—were from big cities (New York, San Francisco, Chicago). They were dying, and they knew it. When they were dying, he realized, all they wanted to do was to come home. Not even certain that they would be accepted, seeking out a "foreigner doctor" for treatment, not even admitting publicly what they were dying from—they just wanted to come home. That struck him, and me, as deeply poignant. In the end, when we are weak, and in some pain, and maybe afraid—that is, dying—we all just want to go home.

The problem with "all who wander are not lost" is that when illness and mortality appear, they want to go home—but do not know how to do so. When you have dedicated your life to exploring, you probably don't know where home is. So people increasingly are attracted to treating dying in the same way that they have treated living—with a focus on freedom, making choices, and being in control of the exploration. With physician-assisted suicide, they are "crafting an end." When you have no home, you build your own house, while you still can. We are self-made women and men. We take care of ourselves. Right?

Of course, as Christians, we say there is a home: and that home is God the Father. Jesus Christ is our guide and mediator, and the Holy Spirit our advocate. But acknowledging that home, through our church, requires hanging up the traveling shoes and

4. Verghese, *My Own Country.*

spending time "with the family." Ultimately, it means allowing God to take care of us rather than create our own end.

This book is written to the traveler, to the spiritually disoriented. I want to tell them about their journey, and to tell them about home. The only key to understanding the journey and the homeland is the human heart.

As Christians, we are well aware of the Scripture "O that today you would listen to his voice! Do not harden your hearts" (Ps 95:7–8). Learning you have limited time to live is undeniably God's voice. Hardening your hearts is being closed to God's revelation in your life: not just about your end of this life, but about the good news of the life in God that comes to those who die in friendship with him. The good news that God is not finished with your life and loves you beyond all knowing, and has the power to turn this difficult time to good.

This book is trying to speak to the human heart, encouraging it to be open to the good news that a natural death will be challenging, but it can also be beautiful. There is no reason to be afraid, take absolute control, and try to "create an end." A natural death is, ultimately, safe, and can lead you into God's life and your destined home.

Physician-assisted suicide and euthanasia are realities that must be addressed through the human heart.

Preface to the Reader
Why Am I Writing this Book to You?

(*One person sits in a room, another enters and looks around:*) **Hello.**

Hello, there. Welcome! And grace and peace to you.

Um, okay.

(*Sits, looks around warily, long pause.*)

Why are we here, exactly?

Oh, aren't you here because I wanted a conversationalist to chat about physician-assisted suicide? One of the most controversial topics of the day, right?

Yeah, controversial. That title wasn't all too subtle. But I'm not sure I agree with you. Assisted suicide seems to make sense in some circumstances.

Really?

Sure. You hear of people having difficult deaths and think . . . it shouldn't have to be this way. There must be a better way. Maybe assisted suicide is it.

I think we can agree on "there should be a better way." But I would hold that assisted suicide is wrong in ways people usually don't think about.

Like what?

Well, I've taught this subject for a while in a theological context. People I teach keep bringing up reasons to support physician-assisted suicide: pain, compassion, autonomy, etc. I think a lot of these challenges may be well-intentioned. But they are not reasons to support assisted suicide. They are rooted in ignorance. And they have "tricks" within them, tricks that appeal to a false understanding of what it means to be human.

"Tricks"?

You know, deceptions. Things that sound true when they aren't.

OK, but—what it means to be human? That sounds pretty philosophical for a political debate and personal decision.

I have a friend, a priest, who has said that in the next fifty years, the question we will all deal with in the Western world is not "What is God?", but instead, the question for debate will be "What is the human being?" Questions persist about both, of course, but I think he is right. Assisted suicide assumes many things about what it means to be human, "tricks of the heart." My aim is to help you make better decisions based on clearing out deceptions.

I'm not sure I'm up for this conversation. I mean, I'm not dying—so what can I have to contribute?

Do you vote?

Yes.

Do you have older family members?

Yes.

Are you going to die someday?

Um. Well, yes.

Then you are as "up" for this conversation as anyone else in the United States. You and this issue will cross paths, so to speak. Besides, you are a living human being. You have some insight into what it means to be human. But it may be a muddled experience, so theology and philosophy helps us see more clearly what it means to be human, to untangle the knots of your experience.

But it's such an emotional issue. People lead with their feelings on this. It's hard to talk about.

It definitely is hard to talk about. I thank for you stepping up, and being willing to do so. But still . . . does it help to *not* talk about it? Or talk about it badly? Clear thinking isn't an enemy of compassion. I hope we can model both in our conversation.

But since I am not dying, I'm not sure I have the *gravitas* to enter this conversation rightly.

I can understand that. But see that shadowy person over there? (*Points in the far distance*).

Yes.

That person there is listening to our conversation, is mortally ill, and thinking about assisted suicide.

(*Pause.*)

That's sobering.

It is. So let's assume he is listening throughout. We are all on the journey together. All we can do is the best we can.

(*Whispering.*) **What do you say?**

Well, how about this? First, to anyone listening to our conversation who has received a terminal diagnosis: I am truly sorry. Virtually no one welcomes a terminal diagnosis. While we are all amateurs when it comes to facing the dying process, we also are all human and know what it means to suffer, and to be afraid. We become less human if we ever lose our empathy for those who suffer.

A lot of this book is about looking closely at stated arguments and at hidden arguments. But point of the book is not to tell you you're going to have to white-knuckle this disease. The purpose is to give you hope. The purpose it to encourage you to take your hard situation to God.

The God word. Is this a theological argument?

It is, because I am making it, and I am a Catholic Christian theologian. But I'm using philosophy, cultural criticism, and public policy research as well. Even medicine. Are you a Christian?

I think I am. Do I need to be for this conversation?

No, you don't. I'm not preparing to assume anything in my presentation. But it's honest to be forthright about where I am; and honest for conversationalists to be open about where they are as well. There are people who can make pure public policy arguments, but this is more of a theological argument. I'm trying to speak to whomever wants to listen.

OK, then. How do we start this?

I have heard five different reasons given by the general public why they would want physician-assisted suicide available. Here (*passing over a sheet*)—what do you think?

(*After a quick read.*) **All those seem like plausible reasons. I've heard people argue for these.**

OK, then we will talk a bit about each reason, one at a time. You ask questions, and push back. I'll close this long conversation with a closing chapter, arguing why you shouldn't kill yourself.

Long conversation, eh? I'll need some coffee to warm myself up for this.

(*Coffee magically appears.*)

Nice stunt.

Last one of the book.

OK, so . . . this conversation we're having. Are you supposed to be Socrates, or something?

Not really. I'm nicer to my conversationalists. Sugar and cream?

No, let me get some straight caffeine in me. You go ahead and start.

Excellent. And if you find any my insights have value, I give all credit to God. Any that ring false, I apologize and take responsibility. As Jesus said, "I am the vine, you are the branches. Those who abide in me and I in them bear much fruit, because apart from me, you can do nothing" (John 15:5).

1

The First Trick of the Heart

"I never wanted to live this way, in this state"

~

How often have we heard this? We look at a person suffering, perhaps bound to a hospital bed, perhaps on a morphine drip, and in frustrated helplessness we mention to another, "I would never want to live that way." Sometimes members of the family, discussing the last days of a loved one, mention that the person dying has uttered that very line, after watching a similar situation unfold on a TV show, or in reference to a friend's troubles, or some such. Even if we thought saying it aloud was unseemly, or impolitic . . . have you thought it yourself? Have you thought "There, but for the grace of God, go I"?

And yet, what happens when you *do* find yourself in that challenging state? Because we all will indeed die. Could "I never wanted to live this way" become "I choose not to live this way"? If someone suggests that you could end your own life, would your words or your thoughts come back to haunt you—or even to tempt you?

I am not going to say that you (or anyone else) should enjoy suffering or confinement. Given many options, no one would choose to live that way as an ideal. But to say that you would not want to live in a compromised manner—one that you in fact have seen but not experienced—does not mean that you do not want to live. What you fear is disintegration, and that is natural, and understandable. I want to talk about what you are losing—and what you are *not* losing—when you face a terminal diagnosis.

And I am here to push you a bit, and ask hard questions. I'm open to listening to you, but I'm not so certain these "tricks of the heart" are tricks. They could just be the truth. And this is too important to not be challenged.

Indeed it is. I hope I am open to all honest questions, and that I take you seriously.

The Integrity of Body and Soul, and the Grief of Disintegration

Sian Beilock, a professor of psychology at the University of Chicago, has written a fascinating book titled *How the Body Knows Its Mind*,[1] a summary of recent work in neuropsychology that implies that the mind does not control the body like a computer controls a mechanical limb: rather, the impact of body on mind and mind on body is integrated and more mutual than we thought. Who knew? Did you know that

* the ability to control individual finger movements and fine motor skills significantly improves math scores—to the point where if people are injured in ways that harm fingers, math abilities take a dive? (And this may be why pianists tend to have excellent math skills?)

* psychiatrists are increasingly using Botox injections around "frown lines" as a way of breaking a person of persistent depression? (The theory is that severely depressed people cannot short-circuit the feed loop of facial muscles "telling" the

1. Beilock, *How the Body Knows Its Mind*, especially chapter 2.

2

mind to be depressed—and the Botox temporarily freezes those muscles, preventing the frown signals.)

* walking, even pacing, demonstrably enhances creative thinking? That walking in nature (as opposed to the city) demonstrably enhances concentration?

* practicing an associated hand motion while memorizing (such as holding a glass of wine while practicing a toast) helps your brain remember the script—because picking up the glass becomes a trigger?

The ongoing research in embodied cognition is uncovering a vast integrated reality of body and mind that we call the human being.

That's pretty amazing stuff.

It is. But to Christians, this integration should not be surprising. We have always held that there is an essential integration between the body and the soul.

For example, in the book of Genesis, the human, Adam, becomes a *nephesh* (Hebrew for a living being, sometimes understood as soul) when God blows the breath (or Spirit) of life into his created muddy form. The Hebrew understanding of the human being is consistently one where life indicates a wholeness of body and spirit. To live is to be an embodied spirit, and the totality of the *nephesh* is named as unequivocally good.

In the New Testament, the human being is still understood as a unity of body and soul: the body good, and the soul, good. It is in the New Testament that it becomes more clear that the death of the body, while not destroying the soul (nothing destroys the spiritual aspect—we may mar it, but we cannot destroy it), is grievously tragic. It is tragic because it is unnatural: as creatures with a physical and spiritual aspect, the body and the soul are not meant to be separated. They exist properly with and for each other. When death is introduced and shaped by Adam and Eve's original sin, what it introduced was the tragedy of disintegration.

Excuse me: death is "the tragedy of disintegration"? That seems—understated. And abstract.

This may sound rather abstract and theoretical, but it is not. We feel "dis-integrated" every time we get the common cold—never mind major illnesses. The body is not working like it was meant to: your nose is clogged and it is hard to breathe, you don't enjoy eating much beyond broth and toast, you may be a twenty-year-old marathoner when in good health but now you feel exhausted just getting out of bed. The wholeness of the body is not felt; it feels like parts of your body are working against each other. And your spiritual life? Well, it is certain that you can pray through a cold. But there is no question that illness has a discernible short-term impact on most people's spiritual lives: harder to focus, harder to pray in known ways. The malfunction of the body requires a re-calibration of the spirit in a way you wouldn't expect—unless you knew, deep down, that body and soul are integrated.[2]

This is why death is seen as a tragedy in the Christian world-view—even though it is the door to life with God, the truest good there is, our original sin made that door different than what it would have been. We *can* die well, loved by God and in friendship with Christ. But the experience of dying involves disintegration, and it is jarring, unnerving, unwanted, and tragic. And this is why the Christian church teaches that at the end of time—the parousia—the final judgment unites the souls of those in friendship with Christ with their transformed (or resurrection) bodies. We were not created for disintegration. But that is what we face in dying: the sorrowful reality of disintegration of body and soul . . . at least for a time.

When we say, "I never wanted to live this way, in this state"—well, God did not originally want that for us either. Yet because

---

2. This integration (and the necessarily tragic nature of disintegration) is also affirmed in Thomas Aquinas's work. Thomas argued that the soul is "the form of the body"—which means the primary organizing principle that integrates the spiritual and physical aspects of the human. He argued that the body's matter is not perfectly continuous (organically, cells produce and die within a person, so the body is not purely static). The soul, as the "first act" and source of identity, coheres the matter of the body into integrated substance. Death is, in fact, that disintegration that Thomas says will be ultimately reintegrated perfectly at the end of time because of the perfectly purified soul in heaven. Nichols, *Death and Afterlife*, 66–67.

of human history, we all face it. And we can face it because *God has shaped that dying in way that is not complete disintegration, an unraveling, permanent end, but simply the beginning of the rest of time.* The process of dying is naturally upsetting. But rightly approached, it can draw us closer to God's own self.

So. God did not intend this disintegration, but our original sin brought it forth. After the fall, God shapes dying as a door to himself.

Right.

But—and I mean no offense—if I were facing death and my impending decline looked really difficult, I still wouldn't want to live that way. I would lose too much—in fact, it would feel like I would lose everything. And if I initiated a physician-assisted suicide, then I wouldn't have to lose so much.

I understand what you are saying. But I want to challenge you a bit here.

What Is "This Way"?

There is a natural reaction of aversion when "things fall apart"—especially when it is your own body. But it is also right to push back on the statement "I never wanted to live this way, in this state." What exactly is "*this way*"? Without being able to walk? With limited memory? With limited abilities to talk?

Sure, let's use those as examples.

While the loss of any of those human functions would naturally cause real grieving and challenges, there is the reality that we don't define what it means to be human—and our right to a natural death—by our functionalities. It is no accident that fifteen disability rights groups have come out swinging against physician-assisted suicide.[3] The most prominent of the groups, Not Dead Yet[4] (deliciously named after a scene in a macabre but slapstick Monty Python movie, where a medieval cart man tries to "hurry along"

3. "Disability Groups Opposed To Assisted Suicide Laws."

4. For more information, please see their website at http://notdeadyet.org/.

those dying of a plague through argument, and finally a hammer to the head), began in Britain and has quickly spread throughout the Western world, advocating in local and national legislatures, writing articles and op-eds, filing legal briefs, and protesting at "right to die" conventions and press conferences. Why? Because they—all these people living with disabilities—rightly perceive that able-bodied people believe living with a disability is literally "a fate worse than death." In fact, they are worried that people living with disabilities will be pressured—by wrongheaded physicians, or family members, or simply society at large—to accept assisted suicide due to their disabilities.

Most people living with disabilities don't want to guilt trip able-bodied people into recognizing a prejudice against people living with disabilities. But they do want people to recognize that although living with a disability has real challenges, people can and do live very full lives with disabilities. There is a profound misunderstanding among most of the population that disability automatically equals misery, when that simply is not true.[5] The possibilities allowing a full life in community have never been greater. And even if your life is very challenged by encroaching disabilities, God is not done working in and through your life. You are still you.

"You are still you"—but . . . am I? I imagine myself confined to bed, unable to talk—I can't even recognize myself. My entire way of being could change.

Possibly. But does your way of life make you who you are?

---

5. Jones, "Assisted Suicide and Euthanasia," 15. This page contains many peer-reviewed sources that debate whether physicians and medical providers can make capable judgments about quality of life issues. The evidence is mixed but trends heavily toward a discernible bias against people with disabilities, and disbelief that they can have a good life. See also Ely, "Sonnet XXX," which challenges the ability of physicians to determine quality of life in care of the dying.

The First Trick of the Heart

Are You Losing What You *Have*, Or Who You *Are*?

You are still you. Ponder that statement. And consider: from your conception, you always were wholly yourself, and you always will be.

> Now the word of the Lord came to me saying, "Before I formed you in the womb I knew you, and before you were born I consecrated you . . ." (Jer 1:4–5).

You are still you. There is an essential "you-ness" that is an irreplaceable expression of the Father's love, and that "you-ness" endures, no matter what.

But when you are facing dying, and the loss of certain kinds of typical functions of the body, perhaps you wonder. In fact, in the face of such a prognosis, people do say "But I won't be me anymore" (see the third trick of the heart in chapter 3).

The challenge here is to see our life as God sees our lives, as unique, irreplaceable, and real—even when physically compromised by illness. God knows what it means to be you, and you are not defined by your ability to do things, or your illness. Loss of function is real and naturally grieved. But you do not lose who you essentially are: a unique son or daughter of God, loved by God, and created to witness to his goodness.

The twentieth century philosopher Gabriel Marcel—perhaps best known as the author of *Being and Having*—was a bit of a prophet in this regard. He argued that *in the modern world, we see human beings as problems to be solved rather than mysteries to be explored*. Problem solving is not a negative in itself—there are, after all, problems to be solved. War. Distribution of goods. Best educational practices. How to farm distressed land. Ethical business practices. And, relevant to our discussion, disease. A diseased body is a problem that medical professionals are called to solve. But the diseased body is only part of who we are. The "you-ness" of the human being recalls the definitive mystery of the human being—that we are more than our "problems." With our increased ability and attention to solving problems, Marcel says, we fail in our humanity if we forget that the human being is a mystery. Each

7

person is an exceedingly deep well who has life beyond our sight, who is a universe unto him or herself. And the depth and mystery of your "you-ness" simply cannot be lost.

Let me put it this way—to twist a line from *Doctor Who*, each human person, like the beloved TARDIS, is "bigger on the inside." Because of your infinite soul, you are bigger than your illness, your abilities, what you have . . . even your mortality. Indeed, you may have problems. But you *are* a mystery to honored. And that mystery, that "you-ness," never ends.

Beyond challenging our temptation to name everything human as a problem, Marcel also challenges us to recognize that a human must be defined by *being* rather than *having*.

Again, that sounds extremely abstract.

But it is not, really. Try this. If you had to introduce yourself to someone, how would you do it?

OK: "Hi, my name is John, and this is my wife, Mary, and my children Ed, Ted, and Zed, and I'm an engineer—I work at Company X."

Anything else?

. . .and . . . I like hiking . . . and the Green Bay Packers.

See, you just used having language! It's usually not as crass as "I'm an important person because I have a great car." When you introduce yourself, notice how you introduce yourself through "haves." Even if you do not use the word, you introduce (define) yourself by your job, by your family (spouse and kids), by your locale, and by your interests (fan of a team, avid birdwatcher, voracious reader, etc.). We tend to present these realities as things we have. And indeed, what we have can go away. That is the nature of having. It is external to us, and could well be temporary.

There are other haves as well—the haves of abilities. We each have abilities—athletic, academic, artistic. We often think of these abilities as defining us. Yet with injury, disease, and simple aging, these abilities can disappear as well.

Marcel argues that while it is inevitable that we "have" certain things, and we can cherish them, and recognize them as gifts and goods—we cannot confuse having for being. What we have (even abilities) does not equal who we are.

Look at the differences below.

There are items we emphasize that suggest a focus on the human as *having*, rather than being:

- What we possess
- What we achieve
- "We have a body" that is ours to control
- We have an age
- We have family and friends
- We define ourselves by what we can accomplish

People who define themselves in this way tend to understand their humanity as something to be grasped, enjoyed, and possessed.

Then there are items we emphasize that suggest a focus on the human as *being*, rather than having:

- Who we are before we buy anything
- Our moral character
- "I am a body" (which is a gift)
- I am young, older, in-between
- I am person who loves others and is loved
- We define ourselves by who we are before we name any abilities, accomplishments, and accessories

People who define themselves in this way tend to understand their humanity as something to be cherished, but shared—there is a disposition of openness and generosity to others, because their self-definition is anchored in something (or someone) who cannot be lost or taken away.

One of the most difficult challenges of our lives is letting go of what we have. It requires a vulnerability that we are accustomed to shielding with an identity that can be lost. And when it is lost, we're unsure what, if anything, is left. We're unsure what our "you-ness" is.

Finally: Marcel makes it a little more challenging yet. Remember that intricate, amazing, God-designed integrality of body and soul to which the Hebrew and Christian traditions give witness? Marcel holds that this is true as well. Therefore, whether the body is diseased or not, Marcel argues that I do not *have* a body. Instead, I *am* bodily. The unity of body and soul is the very form of our being. So, when the body begins to "dis-integrate"—temporarily or in the dying process—I cannot just say I had a body, but it is failing me, so I will end its misery. I cannot separate my person like this. I should realize that when I deliberately and with full knowledge kill the body, I do not release the soul. I mortally wound it.

The Problem with *Million Dollar Baby*

Defining you-ness as something you *have* is clearly portrayed in the classic movie that most PAS supporters reference as a reasonable application of euthanasia: Clint Eastwood's *Million Dollar Baby*.

I love that movie. And it's a good argument for euthanasia, too.

It's powerfully rendered, but let's unpack this plot a bit. Frankie (played by Clint Eastwood) is a wizened old trainer, one of the best, who has a habit of overprotecting his boxers. Scrap (Morgan Freeman) is a former fighter, helping out at Frankie's gym, and the film's somber narrator. Maggie (Hilary Swank) is a poor young woman from Missouri who finds herself in LA desperately wanting to do the one thing she has been good at all her life—fighting. Physically fighting, fighting for respect, fighting to survive. Frankie takes over her training, and she develops into a spectacular, gutsy fighter. It's a movie about boxing, dreams, respect, relationships, and forgiveness. And, in the end, it is a movie about assisted suicide. When Maggie's neck is broken due to an illegal punch at a championship match, she becomes a paraplegic.

Weeks later—at Maggie's insistent request, and after considerable inner turmoil—Frankie ends her life.

The theme in this movie is repeated often: in boxing (and in life), "protect yourself." Frankie is obsessed with teaching his fighters to protect themselves (protect your face, your body as you fight, don't take on a fight until your trainer is sure you can win). Frankie lives out his advice on the personal plane as well—he has a troubled relationship with his adult daughter, who will not talk to him. He tries to protect himself from another father-daughter-type relationship by initially refusing to train Maggie, although he sees her talent and needs the money. But he finally agrees. And at the end, when Maggie is injured, Frankie takes on all responsibility for her welfare—organizing her hospital care, finding a good rehab unit, and even talking to her about buying a sip-puff wheelchair, so perhaps she could enroll in a college. But when she talks—pleads—with him to end her life instead, he realizes he cannot "protect himself" from the enormity of this request. After she attempts her own suicide (by severing her tongue), he reluctantly agrees to end her life, and does it.

Maggie, in this movie, wants to end her life because "I can't be like this, Frankie. . . . Not after what I done. I seen the world. People chanted my name. . . . I got what I needed, boss. I got it all. Don't let them keep taking that away from me. Don't let me lie here until I can't hear those people chanting no more." She has nothing to live for, she says, no family to speak of, and it would be better to end it now.

As absolutely heartbreaking as this fictional story is, the movie speaks *entirely* in terms of a human being as defined by what he or she has. Maggie had nothing growing up. Her whole miserable life, she had to fight for respect. When she could no longer physically fight—the one thing she excelled at—she assumed her value and dignity was gone. Of course, nothing could be further from the truth. Frankie and Scrap were devoted to her, regardless of her ability to fight. Maggie had a spirit that went far beyond success in the ring. But all three of them—living by the code of boxing—believed dignity came from winning. As the movie says: "you earn respect by taking it away from someone else." Living by the motto "protect yourself" makes a lot of sense when your dignity and value is something that you have, and can be so easily taken.

But see, this seems like the perfect example of our opening statement: "I never wanted to live like this." Seriously, who would?

The movie carries a huge emotional impact. But—excuse my wordplay—it is a classic sucker punch to the gut.

Of course no one intends to be a paraplegic—mentally healthy people do not want injury. And it takes months to overcome psychologically the trauma of that event. It is a long road and probably the hardest thing anyone would ever have to do. But there were so many possibilities in that movie to challenge Maggie's request to die, and they were never mentioned.

- Frankie could have pointed out Maggie has value beyond boxing. Maggie clearly thinks if she can't physically fight, she is worthless.

- Frankie could have pushed back and said, you have a different fight in your life now, and I'm going to train you for that. I'm not leaving you.

- There isn't a single psych evaluation mentioned in that film (admittedly—it's a film, but . . .). Any hospital worth its salt would provide that and probably on a daily basis following such trauma.

- Maggie fought for respect and friendship and to get the dignity that she didn't get recognized in her childhood. Frankie had a chance to prove she was valuable for herself.

Part of the reason Maggie's injury was so devastating for Frankie was that he prided himself on protecting his boxers, training until you're untouchable and you win. Yet Maggie was brutally injured anyway. Frankie feels like he made Maggie vulnerable, and himself vulnerable, and he can't stand it. But here's the truth: they were both vulnerable anyway; they just didn't know it. That is the nature of life. You can't protect yourself from the truth—that our bodies are limited, get injured, and can die.

Only the truth will set you free. But that requires vulnerability, not protecting yourself, and letting truth tell you what is true about yourself. You are more than what you have or do not have. The truth is that whether you are in good shape or not, you have dignity, you cannot lose that dignity or have it taken away, and you are loved.

But . . . this still feels extremely abstract. We are talking about dying here. I simply cannot imagine anything more concrete, more emotionally and physically felt.

Well, I'm arguing against intentionally ending someone's else life, or your own. If you follow through with that act, it will be concrete, as well as emotionally and physically felt. You just can't escape the physical reality of dying. PAS is just as physical and emotional. It has the added challenge of being unethical.

We could all say, at some point, "I never wanted to live like this." But we cannot erase our brokenness by ending our lives. That rejects the story that is the truth of your life, and rejects any possibilities God has for your life. We cannot choose to create a new story, a different ending, by trying to erase the past and present. It is simply not truthful, and only the truth sets you free.

Weakness Is a Place For God to Break Through

"I never wanted to live this way, in this state" could be a statement borne of the unsettling reality of disintegration. It could be a statement that focuses on what we have rather than who we are. It could be a statement of fear of vulnerability, fear of facing a basic truth about who we are.

Or, it could be a basic statement that we fear weakness.

Fear weakness? How about just "don't like it"?

I think it is more than that—weakness is barely tolerated in our culture. Where does our society extol weakness? I'm struggling to think of even one example. We value strength, success, achievement. We throw parades for winning teams, we put our most accomplished students on honor rolls, we marvel at extraordinary successes in the workplace, the concert hall, the art gallery, the hunting grounds. No one values weakness. Except, actually, God.

God values weakness. Do you know why God values weakness? God values weakness as an opportunity to get in your heart. Weak people tend to be aware of their need for God. Strong people need God just as much, but often are blinded to it.

A priest friend of mine was listening to me once, as I was frustrated with my ongoing helplessness to effect change in an area of my life. I was haunted by the appearance of my competence—a successful teacher, scholar, happy in my marriage and family life. Yet I was keenly aware of my helplessness, my inability to do this one thing I wanted to do. I was frustrated by my weakness, and my inability to do what I most wanted. He smiled and was silent for a moment. Then he responded, not with sympathy, and not with a new "how-to" plan. He said, "Your weakness provides a place for God to break in, for God's mercy and God's power to animate your life." He paused. "Can you be thankful for your weakness?"

I was a bit stunned. Thankful for my inabilities to do something that really needed doing? I was usually good at "getting things done." It was how I defined myself, in fact. Thankful for weakness?

But that was, of course, exactly right. As Christians, we believe that God is the one who animates our lives. When Paul asked God to remove the thorn in his side, God did not remove it. But he received a word from God: "'My grace is sufficient for you, for power is made perfect in weakness.' So, I will boast all the more gladly of my weaknesses, so that the power of Christ may dwell in me" (2 Cor 12:9).

Weakness may not be a good in itself. But it is not an evil either. We are human, which means we are limited. We cannot do anything and everything we want, even in the "best of times." But as Christians, we want to be in friendship with God more than anything else. The only path to doing this is to allow God in . . . which can be easier when we are weak, and we know we need God.

But God is omnipresent—that is, everywhere. And how do you "allow" God in?

We have free will. And we can use that free will to shut God out and say "I'll take care of this myself." And God will honor that decision.

Think of it this way: your ensouled body is a temple of the Holy Spirit. God lives in you, in your baptized soul. That does not change with your illness. The power that sustains your life, and has always sustained your life, is God. As your body breaks down, that dependence on God becomes more and more obvious. As we each move closer to death, the Holy Spirit takes over more obviously, becomes your breath, your heartbeat, and draws your body closer to God. There is a reason people who are dying seem to be impelled to ask forgiveness of others, seek the sacrament of reconciliation (or make other moves to reconciliation with God), and welcome those who have done them wrong. They are, whether they realize it or not, purifying their life with God and others. This is an impulse that comes from the Holy Spirit living within the person, drawing the person to the next life. The weakness and disintegration of the body leads one to God's mercy. The act of dying moves one to relying on God's power, truly, relying on God's life rather than their own.

"I never wanted to live this way, in this state." But if "the way" we see here is a way of weakness, we are seeing the very action of God in our midst. Do you really want to say you never wanted to see God's action in your life? In another's life?

Can you be thankful for your weakness, and see it as a place for God's mercy and power to break through in your life?

2

The Second Trick of the Heart

"I can't face the pain"

~

When I began writing this book, I shared a ride into a nearby city with a friend who is the director of palliative care for a major hospital. She was going to work; I was going to a retreat center two blocks away to start writing this book. Of course, this book came up—and given the push for the legalization of physician-assisted suicide, her work doing pain management with people dying puts her at ground zero in this cultural struggle. After some good discussion on the challenges physician-assisted suicide presents to palliative care medical workers (how this ethically flies in the face of "do no harm," whether there would be conscience protections for medical workers, how this could create more reticence around palliative care workers), we arrived at the hospital. We began walking to the corner where we would part ways, and she said "I just have to tell you something." Long pause. "Susan, I've done this for years now. Years. I promise you—they always say dying is about pain. They want to avoid pain. But it's not about pain. Pain is there, yes, so it gives us something to address, and we *should* address it. But the thing is—they are afraid to die. It's all about fear. They are really afraid. And it makes me angry when I see Christian ministers come into their room and they are afraid too. Shouldn't they, of all people, realize there is nothing to be afraid of? We need to address the fear of dying. It's not really about the pain."

Is PAS Really About The Pain?

I think there is a lot of truth in her statement. A summary report of data based on Oregon's "Death with Dignity Act" implementation—from 1997 until the present, so as thorough as the data can get—does not put pain (or concern about future pain) at the top of the list of reasons that people who chose PAS gave for ending their lives. In fact, it was near the bottom of the list of seven reasons.[1]

Most people (more than 90 percent) said they were choosing to end their lives through PAS because they were "concerned" (the report's language) of losing autonomy, losing their ability to do what makes life enjoyable, losing dignity, losing control of bodily functions, and being a burden to family, friends, and caregivers. This was a report where people could choose to express more than one concern—and even then, pain was far down this list.

But pain is arguably the *primary* reason offered by organizations supporting physician-assisted suicide, what they tend to call "aid in dying." So this statement, "I can't face the pain," is the eminent support for physician-assisted suicide. But it is a trick—both because it is the not the reason most people choose PAS, and because it presumes that there are not medical means available to address the physical pain.

So in this chapter, the "trick of the heart" is about pain—its power and its lie. Because pain can be a real and difficult part of the dying process, we will begin by addressing what can be done through palliative care. Palliative care medical workers argue that,

---

1. Some 24.7 percent of those who requested life-ending medication from a doctor in Oregon between 1998 to 2014 named "inadequate pain control or concern about it" as a reason for choosing PAS. "Oregon's Death With Dignity Act—2014."

if carefully managed, there is no need for anyone to die in pain.[2] But we'll also question the types of pain at play in this debate. For example, when people sympathetic to PAS mention pain, are they also including emotional pain? Spiritual pain? Is loss of autonomy and independence somehow painful? Certainly it can be. But that isn't treated with palliative care. That is treated by human friendship and God.

And I am going to push back a lot more on this "trick." I think unrelieved pain is the strongest argument for physician-assisted suicide.

Go right ahead. I disagree, but I want your questions.

We live in period where people don't have to die in pain. So why should people die in pain?

When it can be prevented, they likely shouldn't die in pain. And it usually can be prevented.[3]

But I can think of examples there that didn't happen. My grandmother died in pain. It was long and drawn-out, really awful to see. I wouldn't wish that on anyone.

I'm sorry. I really am. *Of course* we don't wish that on anyone, and we try to prevent it. But if you want a serious response to this concern, but we're going to have to talk more deliberately about medical care and pain management. Did your grandmother die in a hospice program?

No, I don't think they existed then.

Well, hospice provides for palliative care—some people call it comfort care, or care targeted at alleviating pain—when people are dying. In the United States, under Medicare law, no person may be refused hospice care due to inability to pay when your doctor says you have six months or less to live.[4] That means everyone in the

---

2. For a user-friendly overview, see Doerflinger and Gomez, "Killing the Pain, Not the Patient."

3. For example, see "End of Life."

4. If the terminally ill individual is a Medicare beneficiary, hospice is a covered benefit under Part A. Nearly all states and the District of Columbia cover hospice through Medicaid. See more at "Paying for Hospice: Medicare / Medicaid/More Options."

United States has access to free palliative care at the end of their lives.

Well, why aren't more dying people in hospice?

Great question. But there may be more than you realize. The National Hospice and Palliative Care Organization says that 44.6% of those who die in the United States take advantage of hospice care at the end of their lives.[5] But it's true that people tend to accept hospice care only when they are very close to death—less than a week, even—so perhaps it is not obvious to many how often palliative care is employed.

Less than a week? That doesn't seem like it would help much.

Well, the choice to engage hospice is always up to the patient, or if the patient is unable to make the decision, the immediate family. There are lots of issues there. First, hospice is engaged when the patient admits that he or she is moving from medical care for curing to medical care for pain management. It means admitting that you are dying, which is hard, and depending on the disease, it's not always easy to discern. Many people prefer to fight to the very end, and try every possibility for a cure. Others consider the odds, and decide it would be better to yield to the dying process with deliberateness and planning. Hospice is a real help in that situation. It "works best" when people accept hospice care earlier on in the dying process. If one of the primary issues is to address pain, it is typically easier to prevent pain than manage it—and hospice specializes in this work.

Wait. Does that mean a person can't receive palliative care while actively fighting a serious disease?

No, you can. But in that case, it is not called hospice. Depending on the situation, you may need a referral from another physician, so it is a conversation to have with your doctor. Usually it requires a referral to a palliative care specialist and coordinated care.

But there are people who die in pain now, and hospice exists.

---

5. From "NHPCO Facts and Figures report, Hospice Care in America: 2012."

This is where the conversation gets hard, doesn't it? And pain is a slippery, somewhat subjective reality and case-by-case challenge. But I think there are three responses to your concern: 1) not most, but some people receive inadequate medical care, 2) sometimes pain can be hard to name and treat, and 3) the most difficult pain may not be physical—it may be emotional.

Whenever we are reflecting on the dying of a loved one, it is incredibly hard. Every emotion in the book comes into play. We desperately want to assure that a friend or family member's dying is as good as it can be. But the reality is, it sometimes isn't. Occasionally it is because people just receive sub-par medical care.

In some parts of the country, access to palliative care specialists may be lacking. Most people who work in palliative care note it has been a long road to get their work integrated into hospital referrals. They argue there has been mistrust and confusion about what they provide, both by medical doctors in other fields and by patients. To put it succinctly, patients sometimes don't know about available palliative care options, and that is a tragedy. Whether you choose to employ them or not, ignorance of your medical options prevents you from making best decisions for your care.

A different example of lacking medical care: my father-in-law died after a long and extended decline due to mini-strokes. At one point in his decline, he fell and clearly suffered some injury—he was in a great deal of pain, screaming. My mother-in-law drove him to the nearest hospital emergency room. After waiting too long for a man in extreme pain, he was seen, dismissed, and then sent home as a "not critical case"—because the hospital was undergoing a nurses' strike at the time. He was still screaming in pain. Once home, he began vomiting blood. Family drove him to a different hospital—where he was examined right away—he had broken ribs, and a punctured, partially collapsed lung. We were furious at the first hospital, but the pain here was exacerbated and lengthened by poor medical decisions. When this happens, we (who are not medical experts) feel frustrated and helpless. It can be hard to admit doctors are human and sometimes make bad decisions. And whether they do or not can be hard—even impossible—for family members to discern.

Yet another example that illustrates how difficult it can be to name and address pain: there is a person in the hospital who is dying, and semi-conscious (if that), not verbal. The person rustles in his bed, and has intermittent breathing. An understandably anxious family member rings for the nurse and says he is in pain. When the nurse asks how she knows, she names those markers, her distress evident. The challenge is that there are many possibilities here. The rustling may be self-protective, alleviating bed soreness. Or, indeed, it may be a sign of pain ("walking muscles"). The intermittent breathing may be a common sign of dying. Sometimes it is not painful, but other times it requires palliative treatment.[6] Families are often unnerved by breathing ominously called "the death rattle," which occurs when fluids accumulate in the back of the throat. But that breathing is not painful, just loud. There are many reasons the family members may be convinced that the patient is experiencing pain. But that may or may not be true; in fact, there are studies that conclude direct caregivers tend to have "small to moderate bias" in overestimating symptoms of pain in the patient.[7] Certainly, they should report their concerns, but palliative care professionals consistently say that education of the family is key: ideally, they should be working *together* to gauge the patient's comfort. In short, there are family witnesses who believe the patient is in pain, but that is not always the case. And if the family has left the hospital with the sense that pain was left untreated, this feeds the idea that PAS could be a preferable end to a human life.

The third phenomenon: the biggest problem here is that when people facing a mortal diagnosis say "I can't handle the pain," they are not always talking about the physical pain. They are talking about emotional, even spiritual pain. The founder of

6. Indelicato, "The Advanced Practice Nurse's Role in Palliative Care and the Management of Dyspnea."

7. McPherson et al., "Family Caregivers' Assessment of Symptoms in Patients with Advanced Cancer," 70.

hospice, Cicely Saunders, was years before her time in recognizing that hospice must be designed to address "total pain"—that is, physical pain is only one aspect of pain. Dying always requires leave-taking, transformed relationships—and that is hard. And it must—and can—be addressed.

The Problem of Pain?

C. S. Lewis wrote a classic apologetics text called *The Problem of Pain*. The book is meant to explain the existence of God and the existence of pain—how can a good, all-powerful God exist simultaneously with pain? And, like most who engage in this branch of theology called theodicy, he argues that God does not create pain or inflict pain . . . instead, physical pain exists as a consequence of original sin, the broken relationship between God and humanity. It is not our personal fault, nor is it God's fault, but it is our situation after the fall of humanity.

Of course, there is also the author of Job, who tells us that suffering is no divine retribution, nothing deserved, but a deep mystery that only God understands and we cannot. Bad things *do* happen to good people. And, to pour salt in the wound, good things *do* happen to bad people, at least according to the prophet Jeremiah: "You will be in the right, O Lord, when I lay charges against you; but let me put my case to you. Why does the way of the guilty prosper? Why do all who are treacherous thrive?" (Jer 12:1). It's hard to bear from our human perspective.

But all of these dilemmas, to a greater or lesser degree, focus on physical pain alone, excluding the emotional. It is puzzling as to why. But there is one theologian who tackles both the physical and emotional—even spiritual—pain of dying, not by placing the burden on God, but by focusing on how the human being responds to death. Arthur McGill challenges the modern ambition to avoid dying.

The Second Trick of the Heart
The American Ethic of Avoiding Dying

Avoid dying? That seems like common sense. What, he's advocating walking into a car's path or something?

Well, when it comes to things like taking reasonable precautions, absolutely, you should. You honor the value of your own life when you do that. You want to avoid dying if you reasonably can. But that needs to be tempered with the recognition that life as we experience it does have an end. And McGill argues that we Americans act in ways that avoid admitting an end, vigorously upholding an ethic of avoidance of death.

What does ethics have to do with it?

Ethics is what we are supposed to do, the call to do the good, yes? He means that American culture has said that the highest good is to pretend death doesn't exist.

But . . . it does. Hospitals, funeral homes, the news. People witness death all the time.

Death does occur, but here is where he would disagree . . . people do *not* witness death all the time. In fact, we go to great lengths to avoid seeing it. Listen:

> As we observe our lives in this country, we cannot help but be struck by the effort Americans make to appear to be full of life. I believe this duty is ingrained deeply into everyone. Only if we can create a life apparently without failure, can we convince ourselves that death is indeed outside, is indeed accidental, is indeed the unthinkable enemy. . . . Consider the American commitment to nice appearances. We often speak of the suburbs in terms of neat and flawless appearances. When we look at the lawns, and the shrubs, and the solid paint of those homes, who can believe the human misery that often goes on within them? And given the fine appearances of the suburbs, who can tolerate the slums of the inner city? After all, there we see life collapsing and going to pieces. Urban renewal is required, not to improve the living conditions of people. . . . Rather, urban renewal is required

in order to remove from the city that visible mark of the failure of life.[8]

And then McGill connects dying with failure:

What about the people who do fail in America? And what about those who collapse of life? What about the sick and the aged and the deformed . . ? Do they not remind us that the marks of death are always working within the fabric of life? No, because, in the United States, deliberately and systematically, with the force of the law itself, we compel all such people to be sequestered where we cannot see them. You'll find no beggars on the streets of America. You'll visit few homes where a very aged person is present and where that person's immanent dying is integrated into the rhythm of family life. . . .

Thus is every American ingrained with the duty to look well, to seem fine, to exclude from the fabric of his or her normal life any evidence of decay and death and hopelessness.[9]

I don't know. Sounds awfully cynical to me.

These quotations were delivered within a series of lectures in 1974. Perhaps things have changed. But you tell me—is it true? Do we avoid seeing dying, and avoid the appearance of dying?

Maybe people naturally don't *want* to see dying.

Heh. See how easy avoidance is? You're avoiding answering my question . . . but yes, there probably is a natural discomfort with disintegration. But now I think we get back to the point of the chapter—that people say they support physician-assisted suicide because "I won't be able to handle the pain." *If we practice an ethic of avoidance of death, then the only way we know how to handle pain is to avoid it.* As we mentioned above, there is good evidence that the worst physical pain can be avoided. But it is almost impossible to avoid the emotional pain of leave-taking. Perhaps that is what those who support PAS think is a "death with dignity": a

---

8. McGill, *Death and Life*, 18–19.

9. Ibid., 19–20.

death that avoids all emotional pain by ending one's own life. It is the ultimate avoidance.

Well. Is that so wrong? Avoiding physical and emotional pain, even if it means ending your own life?
I think every humane person would have empathy for anyone in such a situation. We can understand the fear and the desire to avoid pain. But yes, it is wrong—and maybe not for the reasons you think.

Spiritual directors—people called and trained to help others perceive God's work in their lives—are familiar with this phenomenon called *resistance*. Originally used in psychoanalytic practice, in spiritual direction resistance refers to "dodging God." Janet Ruffing, RSM, argues that even with people who are deeply religious and seeking spiritual direction, resistance is real, common, and "endlessly inventive": "Most of us are engaged in endlessly inventive evasion not only of the implications of spiritual experience, but often, and more confusingly, of the experiences of God that we claim to desire. God gently lures us into intimacy and unexpectedly explodes us into mystery. . . . Most of us lose our nerve somewhere between the lure and the explosion."[10] If that sounds strange, I agree—yet the fear of what God wants of us seems to be so common that our desire for God can be eclipsed by our desire for the status quo. God may change things, and undoubtedly for the better, but we *resist* change: we deny it, ignore it, delay it, all sorts of things. And that resistance is largely subconscious.

Meeting God through the Process of Dying

Dying is a crystallized event where we meet God. Yet we don't think of it that way; we seem to resist that reality. We think of everything we lose—we turn our attention there and blow on the fire of our fear. But loss is not the point of dying—the point is that dying is where we meet God.

---

10. Ruffing, *Spiritual Direction*, 33–34.

If you listen to people who are frequently around others in the process of dying, you'll note common patterns of "God-awareness" when they talk about their work.[11] One is that the process of dying seems to impel people to reconcile, to God and to each other.

People who are dying will often appear to "hold off" their death until they reconcile with a friend or family member, and will usually communicate their desire to "make peace" with a person in direct and indirect ways. If the person dying requests to see an estranged family member, that is pretty direct. Often the desire is indirectly communicated—good hospice workers will note when people are "hanging on" in the dying process and ask if there is anything they need to "move on." And then the desire to see someone comes out. Sometimes it takes asking "is there anyone you want to talk to, or to see?"

Other times people who are dying will say things that don't make simple sense, but are a request for reconciliation: take Andrea, a young mother who was dying of cancer. Her family handled her untimely and tragic death as well as they could, in a straightforward, honest fashion, with the exception of her father-in-law. He loved Andrea and her family but could not get past the anger and injustice of her early death, and unfortunately took his anger out on them, lashing out with every visit. After one event, his son (Andrea's husband) told him not to return until he could be present without anger, and the hospice social worker began working with him on his anger issues. After weeks of his absence, Andrea began to decline rapidly, and in her semi-conscious state she began repeating restlessly, "we *must* go to the park." When the nurse asked what that could mean, her husband offered, "She and Pop used to take the kids to the park all the time. . . . It's Pop she's waiting for." He immediately drove to his father's house and forcibly brought him to her bedside, where he wept in apology and told her he loved her, and he would come every day. She recognized him

11. Many of these themes are brilliantly explored in Callanan and Kelley, *Final Gifts.*

and received his embrace. Hours later, reconciliation complete, she died peacefully at home, surrounded by her entire family.[12]

This is more than "making nice" in a hard situation. In fact, I'd say this is not human initiative. Where there is reconciliation, Christ is. Christ compels all reconciliation,

> For he is our peace; in his flesh he has made both groups into one and has broken down the dividing wall, that is, the hostility between us. He has abolished the law with its commandments and ordinances, that he might create in himself one new humanity in place of the two, thus making peace, and might reconcile both groups to God in one body through the cross, thus putting to death that hostility through it. (Eph 2:14–16)

We meet God when we act on Christ's inspiration in us to reconcile with others, and experience his peace when he helps us accomplish it.

Of course, there is the important reconciliation with God as well. Catholics understand this reconciliation through the act of confession, and depending on circumstance, the sacramental anointing of the sick. I asked a friend, a priest, if he thought that these sacraments have a particularly profound effect on the dying. He thought about it, and said, "I'll say this: when I am called to minister to a person who is dying, the conversation tends to get deep very quickly. The sense of time is compressed and people tend to be open to the grace God provides. The grace is always there. But the receptivity to it is very high—the grace is received and embraced." In Barbara Shlemon's book *Healing Prayer*, she mentions ministering to a dying man whose anger blocked him from a relationship with God:

> I once cared for a man who was furious with the Lord because, as he described it, "God killed my son in an auto accident." For many years he refused to go to church or permit anyone in his family to discuss religion. He was hospitalized in the final stages of cancer of the bowel when we began to pray that he be reconciled to the Lord.

12. Ibid., 138–40.

His bitterness continued until the night before he died when he finally consented to a visit from the hospital chaplain. Later, he tearfully told his wife, "Honey, I feel such peace. Why didn't I do this years ago?"[13]

He feels peace because he has allowed himself to be forgiven by the Prince of Peace. And that reconciliation eased the dying process into time that was fruitful, not loss.

There are other signs of nearing death awareness as well that point to meeting God. Callanan and Kelley say these are common enough that hospice nurses and family members should be charting these events: The person dying says he or she is preparing for "a trip" (or some other travel metaphor, even suggesting a time when the trip begins—and they are often right), being in the presence of someone we cannot see—a deceased relative, an angel, Mary, Jesus—and seeing a place approaching, defined by light, peace, and warmth.[14] These events occur with or without medication. All of them communicate profound peace, which is mentioned by everyone who has experienced it, as well as those observing the person dying. They are meeting God.

Now, most, if not all, of these things happen toward the end of the dying process. Resistance, or avoidance, happens well before.

So you think that "I can't handle the pain" has something to do with resisting or avoiding the presence of God in the dying process?

In a subconscious manner, yes. I think the concerns about pain are real. But I also think physician-assisted suicide is getting used as a response to take control of a situation full of fears, shutting the possibility of God out. It's the most absolute resistance to God ever.

But I still don't get that. Why would someone want to avoid God?

I know. It doesn't make sense—God *is* the source of all goodness and light and the One who loves you more than you can imagine or understand. But Scripture is replete with people who

13. Ryan, *Healing Prayer*, 62.
14. Callanan and Kelley, *Final Gifts*, Part II.

have tried to avoid God, so we're not alone. Why do we resist? I would say that there are two reasons that are relevant to avoidance of death. One is vulnerability. The other is change. And we're afraid of both.

There is simply no way to meet God without vulnerability, and if our faith is still growing, that is extremely difficult for us. We don't trust God with our darkest places, our doubts, our fears. It risks a great deal to expose them—or, it feels like it a huge risk. It means exposing weakness. And let's be honest, if you make yourself vulnerable, it feels like you are exposing yourself to possible injury. It requires courage and enormous trust. If we allow ourselves to be vulnerable—that is, to present the truth of ourselves—we make room for God, and allow him to heal. But the risk may feel so great, we choose the path of avoidance. We intuit the direction this is going and put the brakes on it before we even think it through, saying "but that may really hurt." We act on our worst fears rather than our best hopes.

The other reason is that dying is a change. Indeed, Scripture says the same thing in John 12:24: "Very truly, I tell you, unless a grain of wheat falls into the earth and dies, it remains just a single grain; but if it dies, it bears much fruit." The Roman Missal opens the funeral mass in the same way: "For your faithful, Lord, life is changed, not ended." Dying is a change, a whole host of mysterious changes: the decline of the body, the moving to a deeper life in God, the changing of all kinds of familial relationships to increased dependence and letting go. And some of that will be difficult. But as John says: it is, in Christ, a good change, a fruitful change. The mystery of death is that we have to accept this change in faith. But change can be frightening, and we avoid it in whatever way we can. Again, we act on our worst fears rather than our best hopes.

I remember meeting with a priest and friend of mine after a series of spiritually forceful incidents—and these were all good spiritual events, but very intense, and required a certain "dying to self." I was absolutely rattled, and scared to reveal the intensity of these events, and what they could mean. He quietly but kindly cut to the chase, asking, "Do you think this is from God?" I said, yes, absolutely. No question at all. "Then why are you afraid?" And I honestly didn't know what to say. After a minute of silence, he said, "Perhaps you're afraid of change." I shook my head and said I had no idea what I was supposed to change, I was already living for God, right? I named everything I was doing. He was quiet again and then mused, "Perhaps you don't like feeling out of control of this situation." And angry and feeling a little trapped at this point, I shouted, who on earth *likes* being out of control? He was taken aback a bit, more quiet, and then he smiled: "Well. I think it bothers *some* people more than others." Like . . . me. Even potential change—if you are not the initiator—means yielding control to God.

People say that the most common phrase in the Gospels is "be not afraid." If nothing else, I think that shows that Christ *knows* we will be afraid. But he tells us we don't need to be, that he will be there and help us through the vulnerability and the change. What feels "out of control" is not beyond the help of God. God is, in fact, in control.

Advice popularly attributed St. John Bosco is especially good:

> When someone is critically ill, I don't tell him to prepare for death, for such an approach would hardly allay his fears. Rather, I insist that we are all in God's Hands, that God is the best Father we could possibly wish for; ever watching over us, ever knowing what is best for us. I urge the patient to abandon himself to Him, just as a child does with his father, and to be tranquil. This allays the patient's fear of death. He is delighted by the thought that his fate is in God's hands and he peacefully waits for God to do as He wills in His infinite goodness.

Perhaps we need to reframe dying, remind people that God is good, God is there, and God will be in control.

OK. And yet. I'm still bothered by the pain—whether it is physical or emotional. I understand you're saying it can be alleviated in most cases. But I am still disturbed.

Good. You should be. That means you're human, and you have a decent sense of empathy and clear-sightedness.

It also means that you see pain as a consequence of the fall, not part of God's original plan for us. Recognizing pain as wrong and tragic is a way of recognizing that this is not what God created the world to be. It is this way not because of God, because of our separation from God. God does not directly inflict pain. Indeed, God is the healer of our broken condition.

But what if suffering can't be eliminated?

Yes—what if. I owe you an honest answer on that, because suffering is real. It can happen. You want to be prepared.

The Meaning of Suffering

So I have a question for you: is suffering meaningless?

Meaningless? I just know it hurts.

Usually, yes. But is it meaningless?

I don't know.

Let me give you an example: a woman gives birth. She may experience pain. She may experience a lot of pain. Reasonable measures are taken to alleviate the pain. Some pain still "breaks through." Maybe a lot of pain. Meaningless?

No, because she is suffering for another person, to help him or her come into the world.

Right.

Plus, the pain may be bad, but not forever.

Well . . . it's the same with dying, you know.

I suppose. But the suffering that comes with dying isn't the same as the suffering of birth.

Not exactly, but . . . maybe more than you think. To suffer means "to undergo." Technically, it doesn't require the experience of pain. It does require submitting to a process that is not completely within your control. The process of giving birth and the process of dying both require yielding to the process . . . that is what it means "to suffer."

Undergoing a process doesn't make it meaningful.

You're right. But we've already noted that although death does not come from God, it does seem to be shaped by God for our good—as a sign that points to life with God. The suffering itself is tragic, but the signs that point to God are more precious than life itself. Perhaps undergoing the process is worth the price of suffering.

There is also something we haven't mentioned: the spiritual power of suffering.

Oh, no. Please don't gift wrap the garbage.

No, I am serious. And I am not saying suffering is meant to be deliberately sought, or that you gain some kind of super power to wield against others. But you *can* choose to share in the suffering of Christ. He suffered, he underwent, the process of dying and did not grasp at control—but he did so not because suffering is good, but because suffering was the road to the redemption of every human being on earth.

I want to tell you the story of Michelle Duppong. Michelle was thirty, an active Catholic who in fact worked for the church in Bismarck, North Dakota as the Adult Faith Formation Coordinator in the diocese. She and her family and friends were shocked to find out she had advanced colon cancer. Michelle, supported by a wide network of friends and family, poured themselves into fighting the cancer through chemo and through prayer, invoking her patron saint, Pier Georgio Frassati (look up his story; it is inspiring stuff). There was a lot of pain involved in going the chemo route—but there was a lot she wanted to live for, as well. I want to share part of her journal (from July 15, 2015)—first, to give you a sense of the pain she was enduring through treatment.

> I apologize for leaving you hanging on the results of my round of chemo last week. It was our shortest trip yet to CTCA [Cancer Treatment Center of America]: arrived late Monday night, chemo on Tuesday, and flight home on Wednesday. I started off Tuesday with a GI appointment to see if the stomach pain was caused by the stents in my bile and pancreatic ducts, but the blood work came back great showing that the stents were working as they ought to have. My doctor ordered an MRI following my chemo treatment in the late afternoon to see if anything showed up on it as the culprit of the pain, but that too

didn't show anything. The MRI results were particularly good to hear as I was nervous from my last scan in May when the doctor told me that something showed up on my liver, but they weren't sure if it was a tumor or not. Last week's MRI made no mention of this. Praise God!!

I experienced more side effects with this round including more nausea (but no vomiting, thankfully), hiccups, some diarrhea, night sweats. Thursday morning I woke up with intermittent chest pain for about 1/2 an hour. Renae gave me nitroglycerin to help with it. It definitely was not to the extent of the chest pain I had with any of my Folfox chemo treatments. Chest pain wasn't a listed side effect on my information sheets on the Irinotecan chemo. I called my care team at CTCA to let them know about it and at first, the nurse was surprised as she had never heard of it being a known side effect, but when she looked it up, sure enough it was listed. It must be very rare. I spoke to my cardiologist and he said I must just be one of these people that's prone to coronary spasms, so I need to take a heart med prior to and during chemo.

After not finding what the stomach pain was caused by, it went away Wednesday. I credit it to the prayers you all are offering along with a visit from a staff member at CTCA who came to pray with me.

Then she moves into a trip to the hospital that becomes a prayer session for another:

Yesterday Mom and I had to run to the hospital in Bismarck due to my PICC line being clogged. After it got treated and opened, we went to visit a dear friend, Delila Mayer, we had heard was in the hospital. Delila too had been diagnosed with colon cancer and was fighting it like a champ with prayer and nutrition, and was found to be in remission. About three weeks ago she came down with a condition that caused numbness beginning with the hands and feet. She went to the hospital in time. She was moved to a nursing home last week. The faith of this woman in unbelievable!! She is a pillar of strength and trust in God!!! She continues to unite her sufferings to Christ's for souls and in reparation for sin. She cannot move her arms or legs but is slowly expected to regain movement—she's now able to wiggle her fingers and toes. Please keep her in your prayers too.

And finally, Michelle closes with the particular insight I want you to notice (italics added):

> This evening I was able to help out a little by shelling some peas from the garden. One of the toughest things for me has been feeling useless, especially when so much work needs to get done around the house and farm. It's been hard not being able to help with things and feeling like I'm pulling others away from the work that needs to be done by my needs. It's funny as I reflect on this along with the words a priest told me at the beginning of my diagnosis in December. *He said, "Michelle, you are now entering into the most powerful position of your life." By being given the opportunity to embrace the Cross and unite it to Christ, the sufferings we experience have great spiritual power even when we feel so powerless physically. I have to trust Jesus that even though I feel so useless at times [that] He is doing great things in and through me.* Praise Him for any and all good that comes out of this!!!
>
> Ad majorem Dei gloriam—All for the greater glory of God!!!
>
> Thank you for your continued prayers, my friends! Peace be with you!!! :)[15]

You are now entering the most powerful position of your life. What a striking statement to hear when you have just been diagnosed with an advanced form of cancer. But as she notes, it is spiritual power, not physical power. If suffering cannot be avoided, one can choose to embrace the cross, and offer the suffering as a prayer. We think of prayer as words. But this is a prayer of the body, a bodily sacrifice to God, joining in some way God sees to fit the sacrifice of the crucified Christ. It doesn't make the suffering any less painful. But the suffering is by no means meaningless. Indeed, this is about the highest meaning any life can have: trust

15. Duppong, Caring Bridge journal, July 15, 2015. Used with the permission of Michelle's family.

in God that what we undergo will be used by God for the benefit of others.

I don't understand how you can pray for healing and also pray to offer your suffering to God. How can you want, or pray, two opposing things at once?

That would be a problem. But prayer for healing and prayer that offers up any suffering for the salvation of others are not in opposition. Take Michelle's example. At that point, her pain and weakness, quite honestly, were coming from the chemo treatment more than the cancer. She offered that pain to God the Father as a bodily prayer, trusting the Father to transform it. But she also prayed for healing, for a miracle. God will heal, because God is a healer (sometimes called the Divine Physician). The trust is that *God chooses the manner and time of the healing*: physical healing now, or physical healing in the life to come. These prayers are like the function of our lungs: we breathe in, praying with trust and humility to receive healing, spiritually and physically. We breathe out, praying with trust and humility to give any physical or emotional challenges to God the Father. To breathe fully, we need to receive and give. These aren't in opposition because the heart of each prayer is trust in God.

This sounds difficult. I'm not sure I'd have that kind of faith. Plus, I'm not even sure I know how to offer suffering to God.

I wouldn't claim it is easy—but at the same time, it's not that hard. As James says, "Draw near to God, and he will draw near to you" (4:8). Faith is not an achievement as much as it is allowing God to enter your life. It can be as simple as "turning everything off" in your head, quieting yourself, and simply saying, God, please help me. Or if you want to be scriptural: Jesus, Son of David, have pity on me.

As for offering suffering to God, again, there is no elaborate ritual. There is simply a decision. Perhaps you can renew that decision daily, in a morning prayer. You could use these words or something similar: Father, I give you any and all unavoidable suffering. Please, add it to the suffering of your Son for the redemption of the world.[16]

If you are praying with or for another who is dying, and you are not sure what to pray for, you can pray to Jesus to pour his life into that person. That puts the Divine Physician in control, and he knows what is needed in that person's life.

And of course, you are not alone. You are never alone. But when you offer your own avoidable suffering to be united with Christ's, you do step into a deeper brotherhood or sisterhood with him. That deepened relationship in itself may change the way a person proceeds through death. In fact, it certainly will.

So we can hope. We can hope a person's death is as gentle as this one:

> I first went the second mile with a friend whose body was full of cancer. We never spoke of death, only of life. And so gentle was her passing into that Life that she knew no pain. In fact, five days before she died I found her in her kitchen, peeling asparagus. Her last words to me, simple, homely words, spoken in dying, were these: "Agnes, I feel fine, only I can't breathe very well. As soon as I get over this funny feeling in my chest, I'm going to be all right." And so she was, for she slipped into heaven as gently as a child going to sleep. When she got over that funny feeling in her chest, she was a new and radiant life, and she was indeed all right.[17]

---

16. The relevant scriptural reference is Colossians 1:24: "I am now rejoicing in my sufferings for your sake, and in my flesh I am completing what is lacking in Christ's afflictions for the sake of his body, that is, the church." Catholics often interpret that line as an invitation by Christ to participate in his redemptive work. And if you are inclined to think this is all about glorifying physical pain, recall that Jesus pleaded in prayer to "let this cup pass" from him, but embraced the will of the Father. Also, the emotional pain of his closest friends, his disciples denying him in earshot, had to have been painful, as was the sense of abandonment named on the cross: "My God, my God, why have you abandoned me?" But these examples underline that suffering as an element in the divine act of redemption is not gilded sham but a sustained, voluntary act of sheer faith, hope, and love.

17. Sanford, *The Healing Light*, 138–39.

Or perhaps a person's dying is marked more by pain, voluntarily offered for others—the most spiritually powerful prayer that exists, a prayer beyond words, a deeper walk with the crucified Christ.

The challenge of Christianity is that both are possible, and as long as we allow God into the process, as St. Catherine of Siena said: "All the way to heaven is heaven, because Jesus said, I am the Way."

The best way to maintain control in a difficult, scary situation—and dying can be that—is to give it to God.

3

The Third Trick of the Heart

"My mind is going, and I won't be me anymore"

≈

Many years ago, I was at an academic conference of religion and theology professors, in a crowded session of perhaps 300 scholars, and listening to well-known theologian Stanley Hauerwas deliver a paper titled "A Theology of Alzheimer's Disease." A lot of people would go hear Hauerwas speak on his dog Fido if given the chance, but there was clear interest in the topic. I do not recall the theological details of the presentation, other than it was classic Hauerwas, hard-hitting, straight-talking, trust in God, and arguing that Alzheimer's challenges us to allow God to be in control. But I will never forget the reaction. When he ended the talk, I looked around, and many of these academics were *crying*. Trust me that this is unusual—in fact, I have never seen it at any other conference. We tend to come ready to argue, debate—academic conferences remind me of intellectual fencing competitions, where our foils are interpretations of texts. But everyone at this academic presentation clapped, cried, and some even gave him a standing ovation. Why? I can only guess. But I suspect the dementia that comes with Alzheimer's disease is the scariest way of living and dying that scholars—people who live by their sharp minds—can possibly imagine. Hauerwas was characteristically smart as a whip but not engaging in fence-play: he was ministering to the academics with that paper.

Of course, it's not just academics who fear dementia. Roger Rosenblatt wrote a famous piece in *Time* on his mother's passing due to Alzheimer's with an arresting opening line: "My mother died last week, 17 years too late."[1] And there is the 2014 Academy Award-winning movie *Still Alice*, about a fictional woman (a linguistics professor at Harvard, of course) diagnosed with early onset Alzheimer's at fifty. It is heartbreaking to watch.[2] Susan Sontag wrote pioneering books in the 1970s and early 1990s, *Illness as Metaphor* and *AIDS and Its Metaphors,* as a way of critically examining the way we use and used language around cancer, and later, AIDS and HIV infection. She mentions that every age has its "terror disease," where the illness becomes much more than a physical ailment to be addressed but has this ontological thrust as well that changes and isolates the person.[3] I would vote that Alzheimer's has become this age's terror disease. There are people who clearly think that losing intellectual acuity is a loss of self, even a loss of being. And this is wrong.

1. Rosenblatt, "The Disease That Takes Your Breath Away." 2001, http://content.time.com/time/magazine/article/0,9171,999776,00.html .

2. Indeed, the suicide question plays a role in this movie as well, when Alice (played by Julianne Moore) creates a video for her future self to watch, where she tells herself that she must take all the pills in a bottle in a private drawer, don't tell anyone, just do it. As it turns out, she does not—because she sees the video later and doesn't understand the instructions. But many viewers found it the most morally intense and disturbing scene of the movie. For example, see the following discussion thread at IMDB: http://www.imdb.com/title/tt3316960/board/nest/243051754?ref_=tt_bd_2.

3. Sontag, *Illness As Metaphor; and, AIDS and Its Metaphors*, especially 120–26. As she says on 126: "The metaphorized illnesses that haunt the collective imagination are all hard deaths, or envisaged as such. Being deadly is not in itself enough to produce terror."

Whether People With Dementia Understand Who They Are

Wait. If a person has serious dementia, they don't even know who they are. If you don't know who you are, how can you be yourself?

That is an excellent question that really gets to the point. I need to address some of your presumptions about dementia first, though. How do *you* know that they don't know who they are?

Well . . . I understand that people with advanced dementia don't recognize others, even a spouse or their own children.

That can happen. Yet people living with dementia do remember other things. Long-term memory tends to be retained, so people may remember friends from childhood clearly. Some hospice chaplains know that even those who have the most difficulty communicating respond with recognition to songs they know—so they sing. There is no question that Alzheimer's brings forth mental confusion. But it is often spotty, and you really cannot say with certainty that the person will not intellectually know, at some level, who he or she is.

Alzheimer's and other forms of dementia can be incredibly hard on the people closest to the one with the illness—it is tough to not be recognized by someone you love. But after a point, that is harder on the family than the one with the disease.

Beverly Bigtree Murphy, whose husband Tom died of early onset Alzheimer's soon after they were married, says she was often asked if it bothered her that her husband didn't know who she was toward the end of his illness. She responded, "It was more important to me that he knew he was loved."[4] She focused on that—and it is a beautiful response.

If you're in a coma, you don't know who you are.

Oh, I wouldn't agree with that at all. Far too many people have been in comas and have recovered to say they heard and understood a lot—even everything—that was said in their presence.

---

4. Murphy, *he used to be Somebody*. The quotation is from the author's website, http://bigtreemurphy.com .

They may be confused and unable to verbally respond, but they understand what is going on. **Hmm. But there are diseases that do take away your memory. Brain cancer, for example. You could use the same argument, without the question of how much memory a person has.** OK. Let's assume that there are diseases that do take your memory completely. I think they are rare, but let's assume it.

Is Assisted Suicide Just Ending A Person Who Doesn't Really Exist Anyway?

I want to look at an op-ed piece that was initially published in the *Los Angeles Times* that assumes this position, that losing memory and ability to think merits assisted suicide. This was written a few years ago by Anne Lamott, a popular writer living in California. It is worth reading in its entirety,[5] but I will include the salient excerpts here:

> THE MAN I KILLED did not want to die, but he no longer felt he had much of a choice. He had gone from being tall and strapping, full of appetites and a brilliant manner of speech, to a skeleton, weak and full of messy needs.
>
> He and his wife still loved each other very much, but he'd lost the ability to do the things he had most loved to share during their 30 years together: to cook and overeat, hike and travel. He had always been passionately literary, but he was losing the ability to read and write, which had defined his life. Both elegant and down-to-earth, with lifelong depression and a rich, crabby sense of humor, he was 60 when he was diagnosed with cancer.
>
> . . .
>
> Everyone recommended that he contact a hospice provider to help with pain management, but this was not his way. He said that if it was just his body deserting him, maybe. But his mind? His ideas? His self?
>
> . . .

5. Lamott, *Grace (Eventually)*, 91–98.

At first, opiates diminished the pain without muddying his mind, which was as finely tuned as a melancholy thoroughbred's. But then he began to space out a little more often, and he became terrified by the prospects. One day over lunch, I told him that if he ever experienced too much pain or diminishment, I would try to help him die on his own terms, if he wanted.

. . .

Nothing more was said until one day several months later when Mel and Joanne turned to me at dinner one night. . . . "I won't be me for much longer," Mel said. . . .

A month later, Joanne called to see if I could come to their house the following night. . . .

He was in the kitchen when I arrived, very thin and weak, but still definitely Mel. . . . We shared our favorite stories. He was absolutely clear as a bell, brilliant as ever. Everybody cried a little, but not at the same time. . . .

He grimaced when I fed it to him, like a child swallowing medicine. . . .

After a while, Mel looked around, half smiled and fell asleep. People got up to stretch, for wine or water, or to change albums. He breathed so quietly, for so long, that when he finally stopped, we all strained to hear the sound.

That's extremely intense.

Yes, it is.

But isn't it just helping someone who is suffering?

No. Hear me out: I can understand wanting to help a friend who is suffering. I hope every Christian, indeed every human being can understand that. It is certainly the way of Jesus, who never turned away a person who cried for help. But this *apologia* for assisted suicide is not a simple response to suffering—it is an argument that denies the value of a person who is losing his mental abilities. Remember? ". . . [H]e was losing the ability to read and write, which had defined his life. . . . He said that if it was just his body deserting him, maybe. But his mind? His ideas? His self?" It doesn't matter that Mel seems to be the one who is denying the future value of his life with mental challenges. Lamott is agreeing

without reserve and framing his decision to engage assisted suicide entirely in that light: that losing his mind meant losing both
his self and any meaning to his life. The essay goes on multiple
times to say Mel would no longer soon be himself. And that pros-
pect pained Lamott and perhaps frightened Mel . . . so she offered
to help him "end life on his own terms."

Here's what I wonder, with sadness. What would have happened had Mel continued to live until his natural death? OK, let's
get it out there: let's assume given the nature of his disease he
would have been mentally absent at the end, and yes, that would
have been terribly hard, maybe the hardest reality of his life. He
would have needed the constant care of others for feeding, toilet-
ing, bathing, and medication for comfort. Twenty-four–hour care.
Yes.

But this man, who Lamott says dealt with lifelong depression—and a symptom of that is an inability to feel loved—would
have had love lavished on him in the most concrete ways. Maybe,
mental constructs frayed, he would have felt loved in a way he
couldn't before. If people responded by saying "I love you and will
help you live and die as well as possible, because no matter what
happens, you are so much more than your mind, your ideas, your
'self'? Your goodness is not qualified by what you can do . . . ."
What would have happened? Another symptom of depression is
the constant questioning of whether your life has meaning. What
would have happened if people said and did the hard thing: Mel,
I will stand by you throughout this passage because you are you,
you have meaning to me and to God, no matter what this disease
does to your body? Would something have clicked? Would it have
been a witness, a pointing to our dependence on the goodness of
God? The thing is, with assisted suicide, you'll never know. And
although Lamott may not have meant it this way, what does it say
when you agree with a person that his life is defined what he can
do, to the point of ending it when he's not as productive anymore?
Is this what human beings are essentially about—production?

But Mel requested this. It was his choice.

That's true. We do have the freedom to choose. But choices have consequences. I'm not going to say Mel knowingly committed an ultimate rejection of God in choosing to end his life before his time, because I cannot know whether he fully understood what he was doing there. Who knows?—not me, certainly, only God. But choosing to end his life through assisted suicide had consequences that we *can* know. We can know the lingering uncertainty of which possibilities (and yes, life still has rich possibilities even on your deathbed) were closed off through this act. Who knows what love was unexpressed? And when Lamott describes Mel's death, there are missing pieces —where are his adult children? Or other friends who may have thought there were still months to live, to connect? Lamott herself argues an experience of Jesus Christ changed her life in some very bleak times. He gave her meaning and hope in the midst of some very thick, confusing darkness. How do we know that Mel wouldn't have been given that grace as well? Do we assume God wouldn't have given it?

I'm recalling two other lines from different books Lamott has written: one is "God loves us exactly where we are, and God loves us too much leave us in that place,"[6] and the culminating line of her conversion, after sensing Jesus' presence for days: "**** it, I quit. . . . You can come in."[7] When someone close to me is suffering or dying, I invite (in fact, beg) Jesus to "come in." If I could, I would remind him or her that God loves us too much to leave us in this hard place and then pray that God will help us see where he is in this, and help my dying friend have courage and peace and new life. That seems to me to be a choice worth encouraging, because it is a choice open to God's action in the world.

What I wish people would see is that dying can be hard, especially when it entails losing your cognitive abilities—but even then, it can also be a place where God is especially present, the veil lifted.[8] A person never loses who he or she is in that loss. God

---

6. Lamott, *Traveling Mercies*, 157.

7. Ibid., 50.

8. Shortly before turning in this manuscript, Lamott published a moving essay on her public Facebook page on the natural death of a very close friend,

meets the wholeness of each person in his dying and knows who he is. Perhaps it is less important that you know who you are, more important that *God* knows who you are.

What is missing from this essay justifying assisted suicide is any meaningful sense of death with dignity.

What Exactly Is A "Death With Dignity"?

What do you mean? Isn't that phrase the hallmark of the assisted suicide movement?

It is. But it misunderstands what dignity is and where it lies.

Human dignity is absolutely intrinsic to what it means to be human. It is present from the moment of your conception and for the rest of time. Human dignity denotes your value and worth, and sets you apart from the rest of creation for God and his kingdom. You cannot put it aside, and no one can take it from you.

But: you can act in ways that are not in harmony with your dignity. Every time you sin, you hide your dignity. It does not go away, but it may be smudged, harder to see.

And more importantly with this topic, others can reject your dignity. Every time a person is intentionally harmed, slandered, snubbed, excluded, ignored, and dismissed is a sin against that person's God-given dignity.

---

the comfort of hospice and friendship, and the sacred nature of the dying process. It is only fair to say the tone in that essay was extremely different, and much more open to the presence of God in a natural death. A couple of lines: "I thought I would tell you what I know, because this thing, this aspect of reality, this weird scary aspect of life, can just wreck everything if you don't figure out at some point that it is what makes life so profound, meaningful, rich, complex, wild." And "Every single person I have loved and lost had us around—their most beloved—and had Hospice, had the richest most astonishing love and sense of safety at the end. They had peace, like a river. Even if their death was sudden, Grace always bats last." She closed that essay with "Death? Be as proud as you want: bore me later, because Love is sovereign here. Life never ends. Joy comes in the morning. Glory hallelujah. And let it be so." I do not know if this marks a change in her position on PAS—but it certainly is a recognition of how Spirit-filled the dying process can be. Anne Lamott, Facebook public page, January 15, 2017.

So, if we are going to use the phrase "death with dignity," let's begin by remembering that nothing we undergo will take away our God-given dignity. Nothing. That includes the worst death imaginable. If someone kills you, they are committing a sin against your dignity. But you retain fully your dignity in dying.

I think the way people who support assisted suicide use it means that people deserve a tolerable, comfortable death.

Of course they do, in part. And that should be everyone's common goal. Hospice has done great work in this regard. But difficult deaths are still deaths with dignity. Look at the death of Jesus Christ. That was not tolerable or comfortable—quite the opposite. The executioners explicitly sinned against Jesus' dignity. But on his part, it was a death with dignity nonetheless, even as he was essentially tortured to death in public. Human dignity is intrinsic to the person, period.

The problem is, that phrase isn't *just* a call for better treatment and palliative care for the dying. Most of the time, it is used by people supporting assisted suicide to support ending your own life when it becomes (whatever it means) "undignified."

. . . but you just said that human beings never lose their dignity.

Exactly. That's the problem with their argument.

John Kavanaugh, SJ, a philosopher and medical ethicist, spoke very directly against the idea of someone losing their dignity. When many speak of dignity, they speak of it as a thing acquired or lost; they "[point] either inward to certain subjective attitudes, or outward to extrinsic standards of usefulness, productivity, or measurable achievement."[9] It's fairly simple. First, people tend to say they have dignity based on whether they *feel* like they have dignity. "I feel worthless . . . I have no dignity." Second, people tend to say they have dignity based on what they can't *do*. "I can't work at my job any more, I have no dignity." "I can't cook my own meals any more, I have no dignity." "I can't bathe myself anymore, I have no dignity."

---

9. Kavanaugh, *Who Count As Persons?*, 133.

There may be a lot of difficulty and even tragedy behind these statements that should not be dismissed. But the statements are also wrong, because dignity cannot be acquired or lost. What these statements do is redefine dignity into a quality we have or don't have, and a functionality we engage or cannot engage. And strangely enough, when dignity is redefined that way: no one has dignity.

Wait, no one?

Truly. Kavanaugh continues: "When value or dignity are reduced to subjective attitudes or external qualities, a strange paradox may hit us: Nothing and no one is to be valued for its own sake. No one has dignity; we have only feelings or appearances of dignity. I am a hollow me. . . . Everything of value about us is either how useful we may be or how good we may feel about ourselves. Nothing is worthy of respect. Everything is to be used."[10]

If dignity is defined by fickle feelings and shifting targets, it doesn't objectively exist. It is simply a moving measure of what we want and what we don't want.

There is a great deal that is disturbing about this definition of dignity. Everything boils down to our usefulness. Although there is a sense that each person defines his or own dignity, the reality is that anyone who is not useful becomes, in the eyes of others, someone who has lost dignity. Additionally, the feeling of worthlessness that leads people to assume they have no dignity is often clinical depression—in which case the person should be medically treated, not encouraged to end his or her life. I'll talk a bit about the last concern in chapter 5. But I want to address the poisonous connection between dignity and usefulness.

There are many people who are not very "useful" in our society, that is, they do not contribute to the economy through a job. Perhaps they are mentally ill, or intellectually disabled, or physically disabled. Or just sick. Many people described as such above *do* contribute in economic ways, but let's assume many do not. Christian teaching argues that these people have intrinsic, inviolable dignity regardless of their economic usefulness. But the

10. Ibid., 134.

eugenics movement that blossomed in the United States and Europe in the early 1900s argued that, as these people were a drag on society and without dignity, it was right and good for the country to reject, ignore, and eliminate them. During that period, immigrants who were suspect were turned away at Ellis Island. Many people with disabilities simply didn't receive life-giving treatment that abled people received. Those with intellectual disabilities were often sterilized against their knowledge or will. To see the full flourishing of this movement, look at Nazi Germany. The death camps were highly influenced by eugenics. All the people listed above were among the first to be killed.

Yet there are all kinds of witness that living with people who are vulnerable and more in need of help is actually good for our communities. Many who work with the dying name it life-giving work and a blessing—in fact, this perspective is rampant in the emerging hospice literature. There are similar responses from people who work with L'Arche (an ecclesial movement of household communities of the abled and disabled sharing life together). And beyond what is good for the community, people living with disabilities or with serious illness have dignity whether they are good for someone else or not. They are good in themselves. People living with disabilities often have no feeling of being "undignified"—they can have a rich life, and their dignity shines through in brilliant ways—unless someone tells them, in word or through action, that they are undignified.

Our dignity is a function of our being: who we are, and not what we do. To die with dignity means to die remembering as best we can who we are and whose we are. And those helping us live and die should honor that reality.

OK. But . . . do most people know that? I mean, that they have intrinsic dignity?

That's an interesting question. What do you think?

Hmm. Maybe *some* do, but many do not. The people I know, I don't think they would say they have dignity no matter what. I think it may depend on whether they were feeling successful or confident in what they were doing.

Let me share a story about a person who grew to know her dignity: Josephine Bakhita.[11] This woman was born in Sudan in 1869, and in her childhood, was stolen and sold into slavery within her own country (foreigners living in Sudan practiced slavery). Her slavery, as most are, was extremely abusive. A few years in to her life as a slave, she was sold to an Italian counsel in Khartoum. He was kind and respectful of young Bakhita, and when he had to leave the country two years later, she begged to go to Italy with him (again, as a slave). He agreed and brought her to Italy. A few years later, as a nanny for a related family, she followed her young charge into a Canossian convent in Venice, as the parents were forced to work elsewhere in Italy. It was there Bakhita met the Christian God, "whom she had experienced in her heart without knowing who he was." She chose to be baptized, and often came to the baptismal font, stating "This is where I became a daughter of God!" She told the family who owned her she wished to become a Canossian sister, and they acquiesced. She took religious vows, doing various works within the community, encouraging people to seek God and live with joy, and her reputation for holiness spread throughout the order and the town. She died in 1947.

Now, as a slave, she owned nothing. Her past was so horrific she could never remember her birth name, her present offered her fresh physical abuse every day, and her future was equally bleak. Her life was one of survival. Hope came in a new owner who began to respect her dignity (admittedly, he shouldn't have bought her, but at least when he did he seemed to respect her humanity). And her dignity was fully realized when she encountered God—reputedly speechless after her baptism named her "a daughter of God." Bakhita was by all accounts a kind, virtuous woman and a hard worker, a compassionate presence to many. But she didn't realize her inborn dignity when someone told her she did a good job. She realized she had it—and had always had it—first, when she was

11. For brief biographies, see "Josephine Bakhita," *The Vatican*, and "Josephine Bakhita," *Catholic Online*. There is also a moving reference to her life in section 3 of Benedict XVI's 2007 encyclical *Spe Salvi*.

treated in accordance with her dignity, and most firmly, when she met the source of her dignity: Jesus Christ.

So you asked at the beginning of the chapter: if you don't know who you are, how can you be yourself? It's not about mental function. You are who you are because God made you to be. Your dignity, your value, was there from the beginning and remains there, unchanged, the cornerstone of your existence. Dignity is best realized by knowing whose you are, even if you don't know who you are. And to affirm whose you are means letting God lead in assenting to a natural death. It means letting God in to the present and trusting him with your future.

Who Makes You "You"?
The Sustenance of the Holy Spirit.

Let's return to the trick of the heart of this chapter: "My mind is going and I won't be me much longer." There are legitimate concerns about the challenges of brain injury and disease, but the biggest trick here is that you could ever lose what it means to be "you." Where do you get your "you-ness"? What is the source of your identity? Rosenblatt, Lamott, and others argue it is what you can do—even if that is fully remembering who you are. Kavanaugh, Josephine Bakhita, and I say it is rooted in your intrinsic dignity, whether your brain or body is at full functionality or not.

Those who argue that when the mind goes, the living body should as well, are engaging in the oldest of all bad ideas, and it is called gnosticism. In the very early church, there were Christians who argued that the soul was purely spiritual and good, but the body was an evil container destined to be shed and discarded. For gnostics, the body (and the whole material world) was constitutionally evil, and the human mix of evil body plus good soul was considered unnatural and unstable. Redemption was the release of the soul from the body—that is, death. There was no resurrection of the body in gnostic thought. So if you define your "you-ness" through what you can do, and the body (including the brain) stops functioning the way we expect and want it to, perhaps you will name it as a problem, even an evil, and "release the soul." But this is a heresy in the Christian church.

Gnosticism is a heresy because it denies that the body (and material world) was created good. And further, the body and soul were created by God to exist together, distinct realities, but none the less one demarcates the other, even as they are united. They are joined but unmixed, and not meant to be separated. They exist for each other, because combined they make the person, whose existence points to God.

Injury and disease is a consequence of the original sin. But the injured brain is still created good by God, and to "shut it down" to release the soul goes against the character of the human being. To put it bluntly, you are not releasing the "true you." You are destroying it.

Human dignity is found in the unity of body and soul, both together. It is not just in the soul. Look at how we treat corpses. While there are exceptions, cultures universally have rituals that honor the dead bodies. They are not discarded and left for carrion. That points to a universal sense that there is a dignity of the body, even in death. That living body and living soul, making the unique, unrepeatable person, is where dignity most fully resides.

What makes you "you" is your creation as body and soul, and an intrinsic bearer of human dignity. What gives you life, bringing body and soul together at conception and sustaining you through your lifespan, is the Holy Spirit. *Ruach*, as you may know, is translated "spirit" or "breath." The breath you take is given by the Spirit of God, and animates your body and soul. God gives you life! And as long as that is the case, God is involved in your broken, bodily existence in meaningful ways. God wants you alive until your natural end, and has a mission for your life. Your brain may not understand it. But perhaps your soul will.

Do not allow this trick of the heart to convince you that those living with brain diseases or injuries are less human, or have forfeited their dignity. They are fully human, and they are us. I close with a comment from Danielle Darriet, a primary care physician in France, and specialist in biochemistry and memory:

I am in charge of thirty brain damaged patients. I have always been fascinated by the brain. It is amazing to see how a brain lesion can alter the behavior of a person. But, as a handicapped woman said, "this body is the envelope, do not stop with looking at the outside, but read the letter inside." Five of the patients are in a vegetative state and we can find no way to open the envelope and yet, there is someone there. . . . It is terribly difficult to deal with the disturbing and painful symptoms of people who have brain damage. But are they not symptoms of the limitations we all share? So, the patients show me who I am.[12]

We dehumanize what we fear and those we do not understand. The fault is not with them. The fault is with us. Our value and identity does not lie in brain functionality, and we should not let assisted suicide proponents scare us into agreeing it does.

12. Danielle Darriet, Bulletin, *Institute for Theological Encounter with Science and Technology*, 28, No. 2 (Spring 1997), quoted in Kavanaugh, *Who Count as Persons?*, 156.

4

The Fourth Trick of the Heart

"I don't want to be a burden"

~

"I don't want to be a burden." This trick is so common. But . . .
is it real?

**What do you mean, is it real? Does anyone *want* to be a
burden?**

I'd suppose not. But the question I have in return is . . . what
does that word *burden* mean? A burden is three things: heavy, difficult to bear, and unwanted. The first two are understandably a
sorrow. Life is scattered with heavy realities, and as Scripture says,
we are called to "Bear one another's burdens, and in this way you
will fulfill the law of Christ" (Gal 6:2). Thankfully, that same text
points a way through: we are called to bear one another's burdens.
But the *person* is not the burden. Burdens are lived challenges, but
human beings themselves are never burdens.

And even if you disagree with me on that point, that third
characteristic of a burden is a true trick of the heart: you are not
unwanted. Your life, your self is wanted by God. Even if the circumstances of dying are difficult . . . even if your loved one can

sense some relief after your death that you are no longer suffering, that you are with God . . . why do people universally grieve? Because you were wanted. Because you are missed.

A friend of mine, upon learning I was writing this book, mentioned, "I don't think you know that a few years ago, my father was dying of cancer—and he committed suicide." I responded I didn't, and I was terribly sorry. She was quiet for a moment, and continued, saying he had given broad hints he would do this, and she begged him not to, affirming the family was here for him and would help, they'd get hospice involved. He seemed to acquiesce to her plea, but then a few weeks later, he ended his life. "Here's the thing," she said. "He thought he would be a burden. He seemed to think it would make everything easier for the family if he did this. But he was wrong. This kind of end made it a hundred times worse."

Okay. I can see why *burden* is a complicated term. But still . . . maybe it means that I am dying and I don't want to hurt my family any more than I need to. Maybe I am trying to *protect* my family.

If that's true, that's a noble motive, born of love. But it is still a trick.

How is protecting your family a trick?

It's not. But you are called to protect your family from real, immanent threats, something that is destructive and aiming for your spouse and children. Your natural death is not that.

But it will hurt—you said so yourself. Grieving is universal.

Yes, but as hard as grief is, you cannot protect your family from it. You simply cannot. Dying well—inviting God in, being in reconciled relationship to God, and reconciled to each other—will help. But the only one who can heal grief is God, and you cannot prevent it. Grieving is the flip side of loving. It is evidence of love. You don't wish grief upon your family, but you cannot entirely prevent it. And if handled appropriately, it will not destroy them. You cannot protect them from the consequences of love. And you shouldn't want to.

OK. I just don't know why this all needs to be so difficult.

Hmm. That requires a longer answer.

God's Already Protecting Us: The Sign of Clothing Adam and Eve

Most people know the story of Adam and Eve and the fall. Eve is tempted to be like God, Adam is tempted through Eve, and they do the one thing God tells them not to do. Suddenly, they realize they are naked, and attempt to cover themselves, and to hide. But God knows all things, and they cannot hide . . . and they learn that the consequence of breaking relationship with God is a life marked by death. God is not *inflicting* this on them; this happened when they broke the relationship with God. Death is understood to be a consequence of original sin. It's all so difficult because humanity chose to make it difficult.

What most people do not spend as much time looking at is what follows in Genesis, called the expulsion from Eden: "And the Lord God made garments of skins for the man and for his wife, and clothed them" (3:21). Why is God clothing Adam and Eve? Because they couldn't manage it? No, they had covered themselves. Adam and Eve knew they needed some kind of protection—since they had just acted to make themselves God, they placed themselves outside of God's perfect protection. In their innocence and virtue, they did not need protection: they reflected perfectly God's power and love. But in their sin, they did need protection. Yet the protection they needed was not from God—it is from each other, and the worst consequences of their choices. And God begins protecting them by *clothing* them. It may not sound like much, but how do you feel when you are naked? Vulnerable, perhaps? Then when you are clothed—you feel somewhat relieved, like you can go out and do things, be with others? The clothing language is figurative, but it is also real. Something inside us knows when we are vulnerable and when we are protected. Clothing is connected to that, somehow, and we know it.

This is not the only reference to God clothing humanity. The Apostle Paul reminds the new Christians they have in baptism "put on Christ" (Gal 3:27), and to turn away from all kinds of sin and "put on the Lord Jesus Christ, and make no provision for the flesh, to gratify its desires" (Rom 13:14). And of course, there is the extended metaphor of putting on the full armor of God for spiritual battle: ". . . be strong in the Lord and in the strength of his power. Put on the whole armor of God, so that you may be able to stand against the wiles of the devil" (Eph 6:10, and continues through v. 18). *All* of these images are images of protection against death![1]

Huh, I would have thought the clothing was about modesty.

Well, it is. This could get into a long discussion about human dignity and how we honor it. But it also just as much an act of protection. And there are some connections between the two, although protection and modesty can each stand alone.

But nakedness was understood in the Old Testament as bringing more shame upon the person who sees someone naked than someone who actually is naked.[2] And this wasn't out of prudishness . . . it was out of an awareness that a person who is involuntarily naked is likely very poor, or very sick, and you (the one seeing him or her) have done nothing to clothe that person. Nakedness is a sign of proximity to death. To see someone naked, and do nothing, is a kind of indictment. The prophet Isaiah knew that and used the sign of nakedness as part of his prophetic indictment of the nation of Israel, "walking naked and barefoot" for three years, preaching repentance (Isa 20:1–6).

In short, nakedness is seen not primarily in terms of sexuality, but in terms of vulnerability and the possibility of death. God's first move at protecting us is clothing Adam and Eve.

But the protection doesn't end at clothing:

---

1. It's fascinating to me that many Catholic friends, in times of spiritual and physical trouble, refer to seeking shelter under Mary's mantle, or sense being wrapped in Mary's mantle. Remember the words of the Hail Mary "pray for us now and at the hour of our death." Perhaps the "clothing" is a prayer of protection.

2. Wink, *Engaging the Powers*, 179.

Then the Lord God said, "See, the man has become like one of us, knowing good and evil; and now, he might reach out his hand and take also from the tree of life, and eat, and live forever"—therefore the Lord God sent him forth from the garden of Eden, to till the ground from which he was taken. He drove out the man; and at the east of the garden of Eden he placed the cherubim, and a sword flaming and turning to guard the way to the tree of life. (Gen 3:22–24)

Some people read that and say, "See how vindictive God is? He is *driving* them out of paradise into the cold, cruel world." But he is not! It's clear that in Eden or elsewhere, man will till the ground, and women will have difficulty in childbirth. God is driving Adam and Eve *away* from the tree of life . . . because if humanity ate from that, they would be living with original sin forever. God is protecting them from a never-ending broken life.

I think of those people who have experimented with cryogenic preservation—freezing oneself before death in order to be resuscitated later, in the future. Besides very likely not working, and all the moral questions embedded in the practice, it's an idea that just doesn't appeal to most people. Is more broken life really appealing?

From the immediate aftermath of the fall through the expulsion from Eden—God seeks to protect us.

The Medicinal Shaping of Death by God

Genesis 3:21–24 holds what I call the medicinal shaping of death by God. Death is one of the consequences of the original sin—not what God chose or wanted for humanity, but a result of human action at the beginning of time. God allows death as a natural consequence of that free choice to break from God. But even in that choice, God takes action to preserve us from making sin an eternal choice. He opens the door to dying as an end to broken life, a potential healing.

This is *medicinal*? What does that mean, anyway?

Medicine alleviates symptoms and can heal you. What I mean when I use it this way is that dying is a consequence of original sin—but since "we know that all things work together for good for those who love God, who are called according to his purpose" (Rom 8:28), God can shape our tragedies for our own good. It doesn't make death less tragic. But it does make it, through God's grace, a road to God. The shaping is a bit like taking a poison and turning it into medicine. God shapes the dying process in order to draw us to him, rather than be an end in itself. Think of what medicine often is—many medicines involve toxins that, if one takes the wrong way or takes too much, can kill the patient. But a little bit, in the right way, can cure the patient.

Death is indeed deadly outside of friendship with God. But in friendship with God, dying can be an entry into full communion with God—our created destiny and the greatest happiness we could know—and we can honestly say with St. Paul: "'Death has been swallowed up in victory.' Where, O death, is your victory? Where, O death, is your sting?" (1 Cor 15:54b–55).

This is our protection, as St. Paul concludes: "But thanks be to God, who gives us the victory through our Lord Jesus Christ." (1 Cor 15:57). Our protection comes in Jesus Christ. This medicine protects us from the worst effects of original sin: eternal life separated from God. But the medicine doesn't just "keep us alive," it also draws us to spiritual health. It draws us to God. Dying, through God's grace, is shaped to *draw us to God*.

The early church fathers were immersed in this language. Jesus Christ is called "the Divine Physician," building from a reference in the Gospel of Mark (2:16–17): "When the scribes of the Pharisees saw that he was eating with sinners and tax collectors, they said to his disciples, 'Why does he eat with tax collectors and sinners?' When Jesus heard this, he said to them, 'Those who are well have no need of a physician, but those who are sick; I have come to call not the righteous but sinners.'" Ignatius of Antioch (c. 35–108) calls the Eucharist "the medicine of immortality."[3] The

---

3. Ignatius of Antioch, "Ignatius to the Ephesians," *Early Christian Writings*, 20.2.

Divine Physician becomes our very medicine. Think of what the eucharist is. The dying of Jesus Christ, his body and blood offered to the Father and to us, a union received, a medicine accepted to heal our broken relationship. Eucharist, rightly received, is the one food that leaves us wanting *more*. And that is because it is medicinal. In our brokenness, we are disconnected with God. But as we heal, we become aware of the touch of God in our lives—it's like our spiritual nerves begin to heal. And when you sense that touch, you know you want more, more connection, more harmony with God's will, more union. That you were created for more, and something went wrong, but you are getting better—because of that touch.

Now how can the process of dying be shaped to draw us to God? When we reach our limits, we recognize that God is limitless. When we reach our limits, we recognize that we cannot heal ourselves. When we reach our limits, we look for hope. When we reach our limits, and life begins to hurt in ways we cannot make go away, we look for a greater physician. When we reach our limits, we learn from the Divine Physician there is no way out but through: and he has the best bedside manner, because he not only knows this dying, he has lived this dying.

The Divine Physician may alleviate your suffering, but if there is pain, he will give you the grace to live through it. You do not carry this cross alone. You never have. You do not need to cherish your suffering, whether that is physical, mental, or spiritual: it is healthy to want healing. But if meeting your limit involves some suffering, you can join it with Christ's suffering. That suffering has meaning. Your life has meaning, and your dying has meaning, and your eternal life has meaning. But you have to accept the medicine. It is of no good to you if you leave it on the shelf.

When you accept the medicine of dying with Christ, the process of dying looks different. In fact, it *is* different.

I don't understand how this prevents your dying from being a burden on others.

Well, you just changed the language—and I'm glad of it, by the way. First it was that the dying person was a burden. Now it's the process of dying that is burdensome.

I can accept that there are ethical problems in saying that a person is a burden. But the circumstances of dying are burdensome to others.

It's helpful to look at the common demands of dying in the context of an entire life and our common life together. John Paul II famously said that humanity was created for coexistence.[4] That is, we are not meant to live alone. We are inherently dependent on each other, and that is part of the ecology of life. There are seasons in our lives where we are more dependent and less dependent. In infancy, we're very dependent. Adulthood, usually less so. In aging and dying, there is a greater dependence. Another way to say this is that we are dependent on others, all of us, at different times in our lives, and it is knit into the way we exist. Have you noticed some animals retreat away from others to die? But human beings do not. We have long and thick practices, across many cultures, which other human beings mark and attend and help the dying. Indeed, it is deeply unethical to walk away from a dying person in need—that is the assumed background of the Good Samaritan parable.

This is to say: when those who love you are with you in your dying, I'd prefer you not call it burdensome. It may be difficult at times, and it may be "unwanted" in the details. But call it being human. We are called to be there for each other when others are in need. And most people, once they are able to step back, say it is a privilege to do so.

It is also useful to recall that people helping others die often remember the humor, grace, and the beauty in being present. There are good moments too.

But you keep hearing about caregivers burning out.

That is real. Especially when the disease is very long: Alzheimer's comes to mind. But two things. First, it is possible that a

---

4. ". . . the fundamental dimension of man's existence, which is always a co-existence . . ."—John Paul II, *Crossing the Threshold of Hope*, 35–36.

caregiver burning out is doing it wrong. Please don't get me wrong: I understand that they are sacrificing their lives for the other. Their intentions are good and the act is virtuous. But they simply *cannot* do it alone. They need physical help, and they need to accept help. If there is no physical help, that is an indictment on our society and the community. We need to be proactive, reach out to those doing full time caregiving and make sure they have concrete support. But they also need to allow themselves to be helped—I have also seen people shrug off help, and regardless of how challenging it may be, they need to find a way to accept it.

The other thing that is interesting to me—did you know many languages have no word that translates to "caregiver"?[5] There is not one person in other cultures that takes on primary care of the ill. Instead, it is the entire family—and it is assumed. Americans assume that one person will care for a dying person, and that simply is unfathomable in many other cultures. If the physical and mental needs are extreme, it should be obvious that all the family is called by virtue of their relationship to be on board. That may be difficult in our culture, where people live far away from each other, but that is the ideal we try to approximate.

Naming yourself, or your disease, as a burden to be ended by your own hand does not address the challenge of needing to learn to depend on each other in a culture that discourages care and respect. Burden language just capitulates to a heartless set of values—that when your life becomes difficult to bear, it's time to kill yourself.

5. Buchbinder, "Cultural Traditions and Respect for Elders."

5

The Fifth Trick of the Heart

"I'm dying and I have no interest in going on.
I want to end this now, on my terms"

~

When people say something like this, they think they are being quite practical and logical. Life is near the end, the future is of no interest, and I want out. I want out *my way*. I don't need to see the credits to this movie, so it's time to go.

I'm going to argue this statement has little to nothing to do with logic. It has to do with a loss of hope.

Remembering Hope

"Loss of hope?" You know, even doctors will say things like "his condition is hopeless."

Yes, but they are talking about a medical diagnosis. You are larger than a medical diagnosis. You are you, God is real, and *your future is never hopeless*.

Listen to this beautiful poem titled "Hope" by Lisel Mueller:

It hovers in dark corners
before the lights are turned on,
it shakes sleep from its eyes
and drops from mushroom gills,
it explodes in the starry heads
of dandelions turned sages,
it sticks to the wings of green angels
that sail from the tops of maples.

It sprouts in each occluded eye
of the many-eyed potato,
it lives in each earthworm segment
surviving cruelty,
it is the motion that runs the tail of a dog,
it is the mouth that inflates the lungs
of the child that has just been born.

It is the singular gift
we cannot destroy in ourselves,
the argument that refutes death,
the genius that invents the future,
all we know of God.

It is the serum which makes us swear
not to betray one another;
it is in this poem, trying to speak.[1]

The first fifteen lines of this poem eloquently express examples of hope in the everyday, each one pointing to new life: hope
is a light, a seed, a healing, a voice, and a breath. But the power of
the poem comes in its conclusion: ". . . the singular gift/we cannot
destroy in ourselves,/the argument that refutes death,/the genius
that invents the future,/all we know of God." The gift we cannot
destroy in ourselves, refuting death. This trick of the heart assumes
hope leaves. The truth is that hope is a gift of the Holy Spirit and a
theological virtue. We may ignore it, but it is always there—always.
It is from God, who wants us to live.

---

1. Mueller, *Alive Together*, 103.

"Hope" seems a bit abstract. How can you offer something abstract when people supporting physician-assisted suicide are making a practical argument?

Hope is not abstract at all. It's a choice—choosing life, or choosing death. When you choose life, even in hard circumstances, you are making an act of hope. It helps you see hope. Even when that choosing life ends in a natural death.

The prophet Jeremiah was standing in Jerusalem before its imminent death and destruction by Babylon—preaching repentance and warning, with no one listening—and received this from the Lord:

> For surely I know the plans I have for you, says the Lord, plans for your welfare and not for harm, to give you a future with hope. Then when you call upon me and come and pray to me, I will hear you. When you search for me, you will find me; if you seek me with all your heart, I will let you find me, says the Lord, and I will restore your fortunes and gather you from all the nations and all the places where I have driven you, says the Lord, and I will bring you back to the place from which I sent you into exile. (Jer 29:11–14)

It's a powerful reassurance that offers faithfulness and hope. But not without trials, even the destruction of the beloved Jerusalem. But there is hope to cling to, always. God has good plans for you.

It's got to be hard to "see hope" when you are surrounded by dying, even living it.

No question. And this trick of the heart is clouded not only by difficult circumstances, but also by some mental challenges common to those who are dying. We need to help people who utter this statement see hope, not by saying that their dying isn't so bad, but that despite dying, there is a future with hope.

The challenges this trick of the heart embody are three: discouragement, despair, and depression.

The Fifth Trick of the Heart

Challenge #1: Discouragement

The lightest of the three D's above is discouragement, although true discouragement can be very difficult to bear.

Some of you likely know that the Latin word for heart is *cor*. When we speak of the "tricks of the heart," we cannot help but give direct name to the wounded nature of the human heart: discouragement. *Dis–* is a prefix that means "apart," or "asunder." Discouragement is living with a sundered heart.

We tend to think of discouragement as a mild malady, a wish that did not come true (e.g., "Darn, it would have been nice to achieve that"). Discouragement actually has more impact: to live with a broken heart means to you are questioning meaning, unsure of hope, and tempted to stop trying. Fr. Louis Cameli puts its well:

> Although they generally feel sad, discouraged people are not necessarily depressed. Unlike the acutely depressed, the discouraged are clearly aware of potential and possibility. Precisely because they know what could be, the thwarting or impeding of the possibility weighs down upon them. They seem to replay the myth of Tantalus, the mythic figure who had luscious fruit near him but never within reach. The illness of depression makes decisions for those whom it afflicts. It limits their movement, activity, and their relationships. Discouragement, on the other hand, leads people to make decisions often to stop trying or to pull back or do something else or come to a halt.[2]

The "trick" of the heart in this chapter involves responding to the heart weighed down by discouragement by saying "This is too hard. My rest of my life is already over. God has nothing else to do with my life, in my life. I want to make the decision to end it."

This is a trick that feels like a positive assertion of power but actually is pushing away the promises God made to you. God absolutely has more to do in your life and with your life. Discouragement is natural . . . but it is also addressed in better ways.

---

2. Cameli, *The Devil You Don't Know*, 126.

The most common experience of discouragement comes at the time someone realizes that the medical treatment administered to cure the disease is not working. When a person suffers through chemo to find out that the cancer has not diminished, that person is naturally discouraged. They had hoped, with reason, that the treatment could improve their health. Instead, they are (likely) being handed the news of how many weeks or months they have to live. It is natural to be discouraged. But the only way to move through your discouragement—which may last a while—is to turn your heart to God and ask, "what next?" And that would be a natural time to ask for spiritual help, if you have not already. Contact a priest or minister. They can help you remember God's promise, open your heart to God's grace, and redirect your hope.

Discouragement may be natural, but it can become persistent and lead to a lack of hope. If not treated by handing the discouragement to God, it can become despair.

Challenge #2: Despair

Despair is a much stronger experience and decision than discouragement.

Despair is a decision? When I hear despair, I think of getting stuck down in the muck.

That's an apt image. You cannot get out of despair by yourself, and it's a mess.

Then how is it a decision?

Despair is a rejection of hope. To be in despair means you have given up hope that you can be brought through a situation (like dying) to goodness and light. It means you have rejected God's promises as applying to you, you have rejected God's goodness for you. It's a rare person in despair who shakes a fist skyward and says, "I reject your promises, God!" But people can make decisions that effectively shut God out. Your discouragement is so great you focus on that pain and refuse to give it to God. Perhaps someone offers you a visit from a minister and you say, "I don't need that, I can handle this myself." Perhaps someone offers you sacramental help and you reject it out of anger that God has "failed you" in your health. And once you have said these things and people leave, you realize you're stuck in muck. And you then say, "Fine. I like mud." But you know, deep down, you don't.

It's true that usually despair is something you realize rather slowly. Yet choices are made.

People are open to despair when they reject hope through presumption . . . and perhaps that has been happening for awhile. Perhaps they presume they can take care of things, that once again, they are in control and will get themselves through this. Or perhaps they presume God will "get on board" the train they are driving—that is, they presume in God's mercy without allowing God's will to rule their life. These are also rejections of hope. When your presumptions fall apart, you could be tempted to reject God's promises and prefer nursing your own failure over allowing God to carry you forward. This is despair, and it is a serious sin because it blocks God out.

How does someone get out of despair, if they cannot do it on their own?

God helps. But the person has to accept help.

It can be as simple as responding to a tug at the heart, or the fleeting thought, whispering, "pray." That nudge is the Holy Spirit. The Holy Spirit is the initiator of all prayer.

God can intervene through another person. Rarely will that person say, "You know, you're in despair. Snap out of it." (And if she or he does, it's not helpful.) But don't underestimate the power of kindness. When someone lives with their expectations taken from them, possibly in physical and emotional pain, and holds a battered hope: that person can be deeply appreciative of kindness. But the power of kindness needs to move beyond accompaniment. It needs to point to the source of hope, the gift still shining in the corner of the room: life in God.

Challenge #3: Depression

The third challenge is different than the first two, although there can be overlap, and needs a different treatment altogether. And that is depression, which is a mental illness.

It is no new discovery to doctors that depression is common among the dying. Elisabeth Kübler-Ross names it as one the normal stages of death and dying.[3] Even among the general population, nearly 7 percent of the population lived with major depression in 2015, and nearly another 4 percent lived with dysthymic or bipolar disorder.[4] Depression has sometimes been called the "common cold" of mental illness.

To connect it with the common cold is *not* to say it is not serious. Depression can be deeply debilitating and is never pleasant. It can indeed be the source of suicide. Anyone exhibiting signs of depression should see a counselor or doctor. It is treatable and you have a right to treatment.

The problem is that this makes it sound so simple. Observe symptoms, work with a doctor, get better. Even with a great deal more cultural openness about depression, "silent depression" is still an incredibly big problem. There are people who simply don't know they have it. They assume they've got the blues, and life has been hard lately, and they'll eventually get out of it. Friends and family may not pick up on it—some people with depression are good at "appearing fine" for work and family events. Or—more commonly—they'll know something is wrong, but doubt that anything can be done that will help. Depression saps any initiative to

---

3. Kübler-Ross, *On Death and Dying*.

4. In 2015, 6.7 percent of the US population lived with a major depressive disorder, according to the National Institute of Mental Health. See https://www.nimh.nih.gov/health/statistics/prevalence/major-depression-among-adults.shtml. In addition, another 1.5 percent lives with dysthymic disorder, which is long term low-level depression. See https://www.nimh.nih.gov/health/statistics/prevalence/dysthymic-disorder-among-adults.shtml. Finally, another 2.6 percent of the population lived with bipolar disorder (https://www.nimh.nih.gov/health/statistics/prevalence/bipolar-disorder-among-adults.shtml). Put together, 10.8 percent of the population lived with a depressive or mood disorder last year—over 1 in 10 adults.

get help—thoughts and ideas swirl around and choosing an action feels completely beyond you. All these realities are actually symptoms of the illness, and the hardest part of treating depression is often taking the first step for diagnosis.

The spiritual problem with depression is that it is the mental illness of lies. So much of mental illness is about our ability to discern falsehood from reality, and how the brain malfunctions in ways that trick us. Depression has a lot to do with severely sapped energy and feeling disconnected from others, but becomes deadly in the way it promotes falsehoods.

What do you mean by that?

I mean a lot of the self-talk in depression is manifestly untrue. The person with depression is not intending to lie; it's the disease talking. You feel disconnected from others, like you're in Sylvia Plath's famous "bell jar" looking outside but unable to touch the world and be touched by the world. The feeling often gets expressed in self-talk such as "nobody loves me"—because you cannot feel loved. Or "I'm all alone," because you feel alone—even if you are not. Or "no one would miss me." That's simply not true. If you are familiar with families where a member has died of suicide, you know the unfathomable pain that remains with the surviving family.

We also have to remember that although suicide is a public health crisis, it actually takes a lot for a person to actually do this. It is easier to think about suicide than to commit suicide; we seem to have a disposition to preserve our own life.

Most people who attempt suicide while living with depression (as we know from people who have lived through the attempt) do not do it because they believe no one cares. They do so primarily to escape excruciating mental pain—some liken it to jumping out of a burning building. But the suicide is certainly enabled by the belief that you are unloved, alone, and would not be missed. Suicide is facilitated by lies in your brain. This is a large reason that the Church says that although killing is a grave sin, the suicide of a depressed person bears mitigated (if any) guilt. If you do not understand that what you are doing is wrong, and are confused about reality, you cannot bear guilt for that action. What is between that person and God is only known to them, but there is reason to hope in God's mercy. Nonetheless we try, often quite desperately, to prevent suicide. Depression can and should be treated. But the act of suicide itself is wrong, whether you bear guilt for it or not, and often leaves devastation in its wake.

Now, when a person who is dying contracts depression, he or she may think there is one more "reason" to consider suicide: you going to die soon anyway. Usually we try to prevent suicide, at great lengths, when a person is depressed. Why is this different?

I'm going to guess: it's not.

It's not. It simply doesn't make sense that some people be prevented from committing suicide, and some people be allowed or even somewhat encouraged to do so. Suicide is wrong, or it's not.

But in states where this is legal, isn't it true that doctors are not allowed to provide the drugs that would end a person's life if the person is exhibiting signs of depression?

Sort of. But let's talk about that.

The Problem of Depression Plus Mortal Illness

Let's focus on Oregon. The state of Oregon has the longest track record with legal physician-assisted suicide (since 1997). Oregon's Division of Public Health has also kept excellent records on who has requested PAS, under what circumstances, for which reasons, and whether they consumed the drugs and died.

There have been concerns raised that assessing the psychological threshold of mental health for people requesting PAS is simply not happening. Some, including Herbert Hendin and Kathleen Foley, have argued that Oregon's call to psychiatric evaluation is fundamentally inadequate.[5] First, prescribing doctors are only required to make a psychological or psychiatric evaluation if the requesting patient has a mental illness that "impairs judgment." Hendin and Foley note it is a strange loophole, since most people

5. Hendin and Foley, "Physician-Assisted Suicide in Oregon."

would think that any mental illness would impair judgment. But what this means is that psychological evaluations are not required unless the patient—whom the physician is often meeting for the first time—is exhibiting signs of major mental illness. Indeed, soon after Oregon's Death With Dignity Act was legislated, the records show that about 6 percent of patients requesting drugs to die underwent a psychiatric or psychological evaluation. But as the years have gone on, that number has decreased to 3 percent.[6] That does not even match the percentage of people in the general population in the USA who are diagnosed with a mental illness . . . and it is well established that dying populations have a greater incidence of depression. So clearly people with depression are "getting through the system," are not diagnosed, and receiving drugs for assisted suicide.

But I think people would say, if someone is mentally ill as well as dying, and they want assisted suicide, why not? It's what they want, right?

That's just it. It may *not* be what they want. The Oregon law is a nod to the medical ethics cornerstone that a patient must make major medical decisions freely and with informed consent. If a person lives with depression, his or her take on reality is skewed by the mental illness. It's questionable that a fully free decision can be made, and depression by its very nature impairs judgment. Often people who foresee being unable to make decisions for themselves arrange power of attorney to a relative. But the United States has no practice of allowing a relative to call for the killing of a patient.

Hendin and Foley recount an example in Oregon where an elderly woman was dying, and her caregiver was her adult daughter. The woman and her daughter went to request drugs to commit suicide. The doctor, noticing some hesitation and general confusion on the patient's part, performed a psych evaluation and determined she was too impaired to qualify for physician-assisted suicide. The patient was undisturbed by this news, but the daughter was angry. The patient's health insurance suggested she could undergo a second psych evaluation (much like a second opinion)

6. "Oregon's Death with Dignity Act—2014," 5.

and that evaluation, done remotely, noted no impaired judgment. An administrator at the health insurer determined that the woman was competent, and the drugs were given to the woman's daughter, to wait for "the right time" (there is no timeline to ingest these drugs, or even a requirement to do so). The daughter and her husband went away for a respite week, placing the mother in a nursing home during that time, where she pleaded repeatedly to go home. When she was picked up by her daughter and son-in-law, she said she had thought about staying in the nursing home, but given how expensive that would be decided to end her life instead. When her daughter asked, "When?" She responded, "Now." And hours later, she died.[7]

Did she make free, informed, consent in this situation? The psych evaluation was murky, with two opposing results. The daughter seemed to want her mother to commit suicide, pushing the option more than that mother seemed willing or able to do. And was her actual, sudden decision to end her life—seemingly based on finances and her dependence on a questionable caregiver—really free? Or was there some coercion involved of a confused, elderly woman? Mental illness and possible elder abuse—this doesn't look like the "compassionate choice" some PAS advocates claim it is.

Some other nations—Switzerland, Belgium, the Netherlands—actually allow assisted suicide or euthanasia in people living with mental illness who request it. No psychological check to safeguard free and informed consent is needed. In fact, most who died of assisted suicide in this Belgium study had no mortal disease.[8] It didn't start out that way. It could move in that direction in the USA as well.

But all this rather dire information begs the obvious question: why not treat the depression first? What is the possible harm?

And I guess the patient might say: perhaps there is no harm, but what's the point? I'm dying.

7. Hendin and Foley, "Physician-assisted Suicide in Oregon," 1624–25.

8. Please see one illuminative study from Belgium: Thienpont et al., "Euthanasia Requests, Procedures and Outcomes for 100 Belgian patients Suffering from Psychiatric Disorders."

And I would respond, no, you are alive. You are living and God has a plan for your life. Your life is valuable, and your dignity calls for us to care for you and walk with you on this journey. If you are depressed, we can secure help for that disease. There are many people who meet their dying days with peace and the knowledge they are loved. This is our goal. Your dying is not "a problem to be solved" through physician-assisted suicide. It is a mystery to be lived. And it does not need to be lived through in unalleviated emotional or spiritual pain. We will help you and bring you to the One who helps even more. Because you are alive and because God is, there is hope.

Remember the poem "Hope," which opened this chapter? "It is the serum which makes us swear/not to betray one another"? For those of us who love someone who is depressed and dying, helping the person commit assisted suicide—even if the person requests it—is a betrayal. It is an act against hope and it is a disordered compassion. The person requesting assisted suicide needs your help, your faith. But mostly, they need God's hope.

I am not a psychiatrist or counselor, who would have other concrete recommendations for those people who are depressed (or discouraged or despairing) and dying. If you think you or a loved one is living with depression, I beg you to see a professional. But I can make a few suggestions as a Christian and a spiritual director.

1. Don't feed the suicidal thoughts. If you are having suicidal thoughts, you need to tell your doctor or engage a counselor. It is important that you say this out loud and talk about it. Often bringing these thoughts out into the open makes them evaporate, whereas when hidden, they fester. But if they don't dissipate, you should receive pharmaceutical treatment, or therapy, or both. In any case, if you have a suicidal thought, resolve to seek psychological help, but then put it out of mind and ignore it. Do not entertain it or consider it. Ask God to help you clear your mind. But make the call to a doctor or counselor.

2. Praying with the psalms is a good way to tap into any discouragement or despair, not to mention anger. The psalmists were not shy about getting it out before God. But discouragement and despair tempts a person to dismiss God, and the psalms turn that temptation on its head. The psalms draw God in to your difficult reality and give voice to your need for God. They trust in God—they always end with hope. Flip through the psalms and choose a few, and pray them deliberately. At the end of a psalm, imagine yourself placing that psalm at the feet of the Father. Ask for a response. And wait (the response may not be immediate). If you pay attention, trust me, the conversation that is prayer will continue.

3. "Jesus Christ is the same yesterday, today, and forever" (Heb 13:8). Have you been in a difficulty in the past and asked Jesus to help you? What happened? Did he? If he did then, will he not do so now? Is he not stronger than the power of death? Did he not love you enough to die for you—not just for a vague humanity, but for you? And if you have never asked Jesus for help (sometimes we think we must have but we didn't)—doesn't this seem like the best possible time to ask? Did he leave untouched anyone who asked with a speck of hope? Look at Scripture, how moved he was by pleas for help. If you don't know what to pray or, pray like the blind Bartimaeus, shouting in a Godward direction: "Son of David, have mercy on me!" Remember, Jesus Christ is the same yesterday (in the Gospels), today (as you lay by the side of the road, so to speak), and forever (his care and plan for your life never wanes). Other prayers you could pray, as first acts of hope: God, remind me of your promises. Holy Spirit, give me hope. Jesus, I feel lifeless—pour your life into me. If you are genuinely depressed (or very physically ill), you may have difficulty focusing on prayer. Just repeat one of these phrases, when you can, for a time. Perhaps someone could write it down for you. It doesn't take elaborate ritual to pray. What it takes is a turn of the heart from trickery to hope.

Why Suicide Is Wrong

There is great misunderstanding of the Church's position on those who commit suicide. The most recent catechism provides both direct talk and psychological insight on suicide in general.

> 2280 Everyone is responsible for his life before God who has given it to him. It is God who remains the sovereign Master of life. We are obliged to accept life gratefully and preserve it for his honor and the salvation of our souls. We are stewards, not owners, of the life God has entrusted to us. It is not ours to dispose of.
>
> 2281 Suicide contradicts the natural inclination of the human being to preserve and perpetuate his life. It is gravely contrary to the just love of self. It likewise offends love of neighbor because it unjustly breaks the ties of solidarity with family, nation, and other human societies to which we continue to have obligations. Suicide is contrary to love for the living God.
>
> 2282 If suicide is committed with the intention of setting an example, especially to the young, it also takes on the gravity of scandal. Voluntary co-operation in suicide is contrary to the moral law.
>
> Grave psychological disturbances, anguish, or grave fear of hardship, suffering, or torture can diminish the responsibility of the one committing suicide.
>
> 2283 We should not despair of the eternal salvation of persons who have taken their own lives. By ways known to him alone, God can provide the opportunity for salutary repentance. The Church prays for persons who have taken their own lives.[9]

In short: suicide, like all intentional killing, is wrong. People may misunderstand the gravity of their action—that is, they simply don't see it as wrong. It *is* wrong, but they may not see it that way. For those who have committed suicide, we pray for them. We pray for their families and friends. If they were mentally ill, any responsibility for the act is much diminished. If needed, God can

---

9. *Catechism of the Catholic Church*, § 2280–2283.

provide some kind of opportunity for repentance in a way known to him alone.

But for those deliberately contemplating physician-assisted suicide, with full knowledge that it is wrong, and doing so anyway—we cannot forget that this is an act that is directly contrary to God's will, and breaks a person's relationship to God in a grave manner. But we may better convince them not to commit suicide by entering their situation, seeking solutions to the real problems, being a friend, and offering hope. If you are Christian, your best gift is to lead them to the love of God, to the One who can heal in a way that the most airtight Socratic arguments cannot.

There are acceptable and unacceptable times to offer arguments. But it is always the right time to offer hope.

6

The Medicinal Value of Dying

An Argument for a Natural End to Life

~

Have you ever cared for someone who struggled in life, but was determined to "do it his own way?" One of my favorite movies is what is now an old classic, *A River Runs Through It*. It is the story set in early 1900s Montana, ostensibly about a preacher, his two adult sons, and fly fishing. But it is really about the attempt to explain a death within a family. The narrator tries to explain it through a remembered exploration of space and relationships, lovingly but unflinchingly examining that family's place within the larger environment of newly colonized Montana—the mountains, the wilds, a God-infused universe—and a river runs through it. In the movie based on Norman Maclean's short story, a young Norman (studious, responsible, respectful, loving the river but itching to leave Montana) is frustrated and tormented by his younger brother, Paul, a successful reporter and brilliant fly-fisherman, but wild like his environment, too quick to indulge, party, drink, gamble, and fight. Paul is clearly on a path to an early and untimely death, taking too many chances, and plainly doesn't know it, or at least, doesn't care. Norman and his girlfriend, Jessie, love Paul but don't understand him, and are at their wits' end with Paul's latest close call and refusal of any help. In a key scene, Jessie asks the question that animates the movie: "Why is it the people who need the most help . . . won't take it?"[1]

Flight or Fight . . . or Turn to God

When people are dying, they need help. Human beings do not desire to die alone. Death is not the path God meant for us, but the disintegration, the suffering, the end that is not an end is a result of original sin—when humanity turns away from God. And God's graciousness, his deep and abiding desire to help, to redeem, to carry us through, shapes the dying process into a door to life in heaven. But we need to accept the gift of God's help.

Why is it, when such profound spiritual comfort exists, that so many who are dying are unable to ask for help?

This may be the question of the ages—it applies to almost everyone alive, whether they are actively dying or not. Why do we not believe that God will act in our lives if we invite him to do so?

You have probably heard of the fight or flight response. No doubt some of that is going on. We know how to fight, and our body is actually created to fight infections and disease—that is why we have an immune system. A lot of the challenge of dying well is knowing when to lay down the sword. If it helps, Scripture assures us that God takes up the fight when we cannot: "The Lord will fight for you, and you have only to keep still" (Exod 14:14). But the front of the fight may change—from your physical life to your spiritual life. But you can imagine, even make it a prayer, to hand over your fight to God and let him fight for you.

Flight is actually more spiritually dangerous. We resist and think we don't need that God thing yet, we say it doesn't matter (God's going to do what God's going to do), or we just busy ourselves with distractions. We may be afraid—of admitting this is

1. *A River Runs Through It*, directed by Robert Redford.

dying, of what family or friends may say, of the vulnerability of admitting a need for help, and of giving up control.

Assisted suicide roots its appeal in taking away that fear of giving up control, and offers it back to you on a dressed plate that promises no physical pain. But it is a control that does not help; instead, it hurts. It is a control that aims for a preconceived notion of "safe" and does not invite God's bigger, better, more-phenomenal-than-you-can-imagine plans in. But you need to ask.

And those who are family and friends—you need to offer God. Or offer to bring in someone who can offer God to them.

One of the biggest problems with people weighing the pros and cons of assisted suicide is that they never consider how big God is, how personal God is, how healing God is. Not just on this issue, but often, I encounter the mistaken belief that God is this vague sense of goodness that we completely understand and supports all our actions. I encounter a sense of God that he is a lot like your most loyal, sweet dog. That small God is not the Christian God. It is a fiction of your imagination and a projection based in your need to control, and define what is safe.

I do not mean to sound harsh. I do mean that we should all take a close look at who we think God is, and how deep our desire to control runs. Perhaps you've read C. S. Lewis's *The Lion, The Witch, and The Wardrobe*, and recall the conversation between the children who fell through the wardrobe door into the land of Narnia, who befriended a faun who was then frozen alive by an evil Queen, and their friends the Beavers who are leading them to the one they knew who would help: Aslan, the Great Lion and Lord of the Wood:

> "Ooh," said Susan. "I'd thought he was a man. Is he—quite safe? I shall feel rather nervous about meeting a Lion."
>
> "That you will, dearie, and no mistake," said Mrs. Beaver; "if there's anyone who can appear before Aslan without their knees knocking, they're just braver than most or plain silly."
>
> "Then he isn't safe?" said Lucy?

"Safe?" said Mr. Beaver; "don't you hear what Mrs. Beaver tells you? Who said anything about safe? 'Course he isn't safe. But he's good. He's the King, I tell you."[2]

I don't think people fully appreciate the profound goodness of God, because we—yes, even those of us who define ourselves as devout—tend to treat God as a functionary, as something or someone we can understand and control. God is the One who created us, and can be encountered in ways that change your life. And God is *real*: as real as your illness, and wanting to help you. Is God safe? Well, as the all-powerful one, not necessarily. But if you trust that he is the one who wants you back? Yes—in that sense the safest one you can turn to, and safer than your attempts to control.

The best thing we can do when we are confused, frightened, or in pain is to open ourselves to the reality of God, his power and his love. And there is no question that can be difficult—fear and pain are incredibly distracting. But God is bigger than both, loves you, and wants to help you. But respecting our free will, he hovers and awaits an opening. That opening is asking for his help, asking for him.

What does "opening ourselves to the reality of God" *mean*, though? What does it look like to do that?

I am Catholic. As a Catholic, the first thing I would recommend to someone dying who is considering being "open to God" is to meet the grace of God through the sacramental anointing of the sick. If God is real, and this sacrament is a visible sign of God's invisible grace, then this is how you encounter God. The effects noted in the Catechism are remarkable:

> **1532** The special grace of the sacrament of the Anointing of the Sick has as its effects:
> – the uniting of the sick person to the passion of Christ, for his own good and that of the whole Church;
> – the strengthening, peace, and courage to endure in a Christian manner the sufferings of illness or old age;
> – the forgiveness of sins, if the sick person was not able to obtain it through the sacrament of Penance;

2. Lewis, *The Lion, the Witch, and the Wardrobe*, 79–80.

– the restoration of health, if it is conducive to the salvation of his soul;

– the preparation for passing over to eternal life.[3]

So an openness to receive this sacrament—and it doesn't need to be minutes before your death, whenever you become seriously ill is appropriate—and then receiving it yields meaning, joining with Christ, peace, courage, forgiveness, preparation for heaven, and possibly restoration of health! That's quite the set of promises! And yet the promises are rooted in God's revelation, and they are true. But you need to ask for it. You at least need to ask to see a priest, who will likely offer it.

I will say this, as a person who has received that sacrament and seen others receive it, the sense of peace received can be unbelievable. People describe it like immersing yourself in a spiritual lake—you feel it in your soul and with every nerve of your body. Admittedly not everyone receives it that way; sacraments confer grace regardless of whether you feel it or not (a reassuring point that God's action is greater and more trustworthy than our feelings!). But when people make themselves vulnerable, recognize their weakness, and humbly ask for God's life to rush in (that is what it means to request sacramental anointing), it is remarkable how many report a spiritual consolation that has physical effects.

And what if you are not Catholic? Or you are Catholic and there is no priest around, and the time is now? You pray. It really is as simple as that. You pray as best as you know how, but I would suggest a prayer of openness to God. When people are dying, I pray for Jesus to pour his life into the person. Maybe the Scripture from 2 Corinthians 4:7–15 may help us realize this great exchange:

> . . . But we have this treasure in clay jars, so that it may be made clear that this extraordinary power belongs to God and does not come from us.
>
> We are afflicted in every way, but not crushed; perplexed, but not driven to despair; persecuted, but not forsaken; struck down, but not destroyed; always carrying in the body the death of Jesus, so that the life of Jesus

---

3. *Catechism of the Catholic Church*, § 1532.

may also be made visible in our bodies. *For while we live, we are always being given up to death for Jesus' sake, so that the life of Jesus may be made visible in our mortal flesh.*

So death is at work in us, but life in you. But just as we have the same spirit of faith that is in accordance with scripture—"I believed, and so I spoke"—we also believe, and so we speak, because we know that the one who raised the Lord Jesus will raise us also with Jesus, and will bring us with you into his presence. Yes, everything is for your sake, so that grace, as it extends to more and more people, may increase thanksgiving, to the glory of God. (Italics added.)

I believe our bodies are more than clay jars (so does the writer—this is a metaphor), but it is an important visual icon because *it helps us imagine ourselves as ones who are meant to be filled with the power of God.* In fact, there are many pouring metaphors in Scripture (italicized below):

- Bring the full tithe into the storehouse, so that there may be food in my house, and thus put me to the test, says the Lord of hosts; see if I will not open the windows of heaven for you and *pour down* for you an overflowing blessing (Mal 3:10, Hebrew: *wahariqoti*).

- Then afterward I will *pour out* my spirit on all flesh; your sons and your daughters shall prophesy, your old men shall dream dreams, and your young men shall see visions (Joel 2:28, Hebrew: *shaphak*).

- Do not judge, and you will not be judged; do not condemn, and you will not be condemned. Forgive, and you will be forgiven; give, and it will be given to you. A good measure, pressed down, shaken together, running over, will be put [other translations: *poured*] into your lap; for the measure you give will be the measure you get back (Luke 6:37–38, Greek: *dōsousin*).

- He said to them, "This is my blood of the covenant, which is *poured out* for many" (Mark 14:24, Greek: *ekcheō*; same verb in Matt 26:28, Luke 22:20).

- Being therefore exalted at the right hand of God, and having received from the Father the promise of the Holy Spirit, he has *poured out* this [Pentecost] that you both see and hear (Acts 2:33, Greek: *ekcheō*).

- The circumcised believers who had come with Peter were astounded that the gift of the Holy Spirit had been *poured out* even on the Gentiles (Acts 10:45, Greek: *ekcheō*).

- . . .[H]ope does not disappoint us, because God's love *has been poured into* our hearts through the Holy Spirit that has been given to us (Rom 5:5, Greek: *ekcheō*).

And there are many more. Pouring is a powerfully active word, which indicates generosity, fullness, total giving, releasing, emptying. And as little as we pour out in sacrifice,[4] God fills with his own pouring, beyond imagining. We are meant to receive the pouring out of the Holy Spirit. And there is no better time to remember this than as we are dying.

Indeed, the sacramental anointing—all anointings!—are a pouring out of the Spirit on the person, signed in oil. In ancient times, the oil was *poured* on your forehead. You were created to receive this great exchange that makes you who you really are. Your sacrifice—your dying—takes nothing away from who you are. That's the world talking. But if you can open yourself by a willingness to receive God, a giving or turning of your heart to God, you can receive what is necessary to die well, to meet God, to be at peace, and be who you are.

This is God's promise to you: The Holy Spirit. That is, himself.

> . . . they were cut to the heart and said to Peter and to the other apostles, "Brothers, what should we do?" Peter said to them, "Repent, and be baptized every one of you in the name of Jesus Christ so that your sins may be forgiven; and *you will receive the gift of the Holy Spirit. For the promise is for you, for your children, and for all who*

---

4. For a scriptural example, see 2 Timothy 4:6: "As for me, I am already being poured out as a libation, and the time of my departure has come."

are far away, everyone whom the Lord our God calls to him." (Acts 2:37–39, italics added)

The Holy Spirit is God's promise of power, peace, and courage to live with an illness in a way that does not destroy you, but increases your connection to God and your true self. And God's promises are true. After all, he is the Truth, the Way, and the Life. He is gift to those who open their hands and hearts with good will.

God still has work to do through you in your life

One of the saddest things I hear from people who are aging or ill is the phrase "I'm useless in this condition." It's true that your circle of activity becomes smaller, at least in most cases. And "usefulness" is not the ultimate measure of a person. But oh, you are not useless. You underestimate the power of God and the desire of God to make all things new, to use you in his plan of salvation. Maybe you have fallen victim to the "small god of comfort" syndrome (and trust me—we all do sometimes). But think of sometime in your life when you felt most alive. Was that "comfortable"? Comfort has its place, but it is probably not the right word. But even when you are ill, impaired, or dying—I hope with good palliative care, but even if not—God still has work to do through you in your life.

Remember the story of Michelle, in chapter two. She was told that, largely confined to a bed and weak from chemo and cancer, she was entering the most powerful period of her life. How completely countercultural—but how completely right, in that she began to manifest Christ in her own body through her human weakness welcoming the Spirit of God. She offered her prayers for others and became that living sacrifice. She moved and inspired many to more deeply reach out to God, in her immediate circle and beyond. This is no small thing. In fact, it is *the* thing, if you are willing to trust that God the Father is more than the "small god of comfort," and has a mission of nothing less than save the world.

On a smaller (but still big) scale, many events happen in the last days or weeks of a life that impact the person dying, and his or her family and friends, immensely. Remember Lamott's recounting of her participation in an assisted suicide of her friend "Mel" (chapter 3)? She mentions casually at the beginning of that essay that Mel had dealt with lifelong depression, and was struggling with melancholy in this period of his illness. This would be enough to disqualify Mel from receiving assisted suicide medication in Oregon: there would always be the question of whether or not this was a fully competent decision. But there is also a bigger issue. Mel was facing a challenging death from brain cancer. He was also clearly beloved by his wife and friends. But depression masks this reality, and makes it hard to feel loved. Perhaps—no guarantee, but perhaps—with his mental abilities wearing thin, he would have been able to feel the love that his family and friends would pour on him. The gift of feeling loved. Is there anything more powerful? Especially when you have struggled all your life to feel it?

To give another example of God working through a person's life, even while dying: a friend of mine (let's call her Kate) had a very difficult relationship with her father. Growing up, her father was an alcoholic, and the alcoholism ravaged her family both emotionally and financially. When Kate was a young adult her mother died, and she moved away and had very limited contact with her father, who was sometimes drunk and generally not present. Two decades later, Kate found out her father had Alzheimer's disease. He was living alone with some contact from his children, but not much. Kate decided it would be best to live closer to her father for awhile and help coordinate his care and needs. This was a difficult decision for her—her father had not entirely welcomed her "interference" (getting him to medical appointments, making herself the driver and not him). But she moved there—and after he died a few months later, she returned and said "I never would have expected it. That was a healing time, for both of us. He couldn't remember what I could remember about growing up—he really couldn't—so I had to let it go. It gave us a chance to start over. So we did. He was grateful I was there, in the end, and I realized in the process that I loved him more than I hated what he did." She thought God was asking her to fulfill the fourth commandment (honor your mother and father), but God was calling her to receive the father she had lost. Those months were hard—but they were also a great gift.

And, by the way, since God speaks and touches your spirit, comas are no impediment to God working through your life. You don't need to be awake for God to converse with you. Even in Scripture, God often speaks through dreams. Another friend was in a medically induced coma for days and says she largely understood what was going on for most of it, and had a strong sense of being protected by the mantle of Mary, the Mother of God, allowing her to sleep and recover. She survived the coma (obviously), but that time made a deep impression on her of being protected and loved. There is no way she would say "nothing happened there."

Remember, hospice workers argue it is very typical for people who are dying to seek reconciliation with others—often shocking family members who didn't expect this turn of events, to express love in ways they would previously be uncomfortable offering to others. The impulse seems spontaneous, like a grace given and shared. You probably already know the positive impact that has on those who are left behind. But besides God working for others through your actions, God works on *you*. You may find it hard to believe, but many people dying receive a deep sense of peace and joy. As a woman named Lillian said: "I think I came here, to this hospice, so I could finally experience joy."[5] Do you think that is impossible? It is impossible only if you believe in the small god of comfort rather than the Christian God.

Learning to Let God Be in Control: the Peace of Deep Dependence

So much of what is difficult about dying is handing God the control panel. It is the number one concern registered among people who request physician assisted suicide. We love our freedom—and will cling to it, white knuckled, to the end. But when you exercise

5. Stoddard, *The Hospice Movement*, 212.

your freedom by clinging onto something with all your might—
are you really free anymore? Or are you "caught" by your clinging?

Most Christians have a healthy understanding of free will as
a gift of God, and the call to exercise that free will by making good
choices. But perfect freedom is experienced in directing the gift of
free will toward the will of God. When we freely act in a way that
points us to God, we experience the freedom of being fully ourselves, fully loved. That is, we're not acting like we're in bondage.
As when Jesus says "I no longer call you slaves, but friends" (John
15:15): friends are freely chosen. Slaves have neither freedom nor
intimate knowledge of their master.

When we say we depend on God, and we place ourselves in
his will, we are simply taking our hands off the wheel and "letting God drive" in situations beyond our control. Dying is beyond
our complete control. We can shape it through palliative care and
our own choices. But when we intentionally end our own lives,
we point ourselves away from God's open embrace. We may not
realize the fullness of that act, and therefore may not incur full
culpability. But the act itself is wrong because it moves us away
from God. Another way of saying that is that it is against God's
will. Yet another way of saying that is God wants to meet you, hold
your spirit, and help you—but you are foregoing that in favor of
keeping your tight grip on your own control.

The thing that is hard to imagine—as we focus on loss, fear,
and tightening our grip—is the profound peace that comes with
deep dependence on God. The closest experience some of us will
have had is a child's dependence on a parent—the sense of being
able to sleep because a mother if near, or a situation is safe because
a father is near. Not worrying about when you will eat next because
a parent is providing for you. Not everyone has had that experience of love and security, and I am sorry if you are one of them.
But some have.

Perhaps you can imagine yourself as a feather, lifted on the
wind. Fr. Jean Pierre de Caussade (1675–1751) used this image to
help people imagine what it feels like to depend on God.[6] The wind

6. de Caussade, *Abandonment to Divine Providence*, 81.

is not aimless—it is the Holy Spirit, the Promise of God. And the wind is picking you up and moving you to where you need to be, without any effort from you other than to allow it to happen.

Perhaps the most important thing to realize is that while learning to let God be in control is a lifelong process, the first and most important step is simple. You simply ask God to help you depend on him. You could ask for help in putting your life in his hands.

It is such a grace to realize that you don't have to be in control—and that there is one who is, and only wants what is best for you. Do you remember doing the flexed arm hang in school? It may feel like you've been hanging on to a pull-up bar for far too long, vaguely certain that there is a pool of hot lava underneath that will burn you up if you let go. But then you do let go, and crash to a soft mat—with such intense, indescribable physical relief. Depending on God can be like that—only the relief is primarily spiritual.

Learning to Let God Be the Source of Your Life: The Joy of Letting Yourself Be Loved

Irenaeus of Lyons, a bishop from the second century, wrote: "The glory of God is the human being fully alive." It's a beautiful statement, but one often misunderstood. Let's unpack this a bit.

When have you felt "fully alive"? Think of three or four different options. Think about what made you feel "alive" at that point.

I'm going to name a couple of examples. One example may be engaging in some physical goal, or achievement: let's say a marathon. By definition that is not physically easy, requires self-denial, and work. It may well involve pain, or at least lack of comfort. It also can provide focus, discipline, a reason to get up, and—one assumes—enjoyment! When you pound the pavement and make progress, you feel alive. And frankly, when you are struggling, you still feel alive, not dead. There is something within you that is striving to overcome your limits. That is the aliveness.

Another example is giving birth. I'm going to stick with a supported, natural childbirth (because while c-sections are sometimes necessary, this analogy is not going to work as well with surgical births). Giving birth is hard work—very hard work. All kinds of muscles are working in ways they never have before, for great purpose. It is intense and can be emotionally all over the place. But when approached well—you feel absolutely alive.

Now, in either case, you are not alive thanks to the small god of comfort. You are alive in that your body, in as much as you can muster, is joined with your spirit and the Spirit of God, moving beyond the limits of what sheer effort can do. You are working with the Lord, through your spirit and body, toward transcendence. That is being fully alive.

This is not achievement based, although there can be joy in the achievement. If you twist your ankle on mile twenty and drop out of the marathon, there is disappointment, but hopefully the satisfaction that you tried. If your birth ends up needing medical intervention to ensure a safe delivery, you may be disappointed, but the effort to give birth is not wasted. The aliveness is in the journey, your cooperation with God's will on the journey. That is what being "fully alive" means.

People feel—and are—most fully alive when they allow God to be the source of their lives. That is not just a cognitive acknowledgement that God is the Creator (although you have to start somewhere). That is what happens when you invite and welcome God into your very self.

I remember reading about an agnostic man who attended a praise and worship prayer meeting in a desperately poor community. Seeing all these people, clearly with personal burdens and challenges, come in slumped and beaten, then immediately move into exuberant songs of praise and leave refreshed, was disturbing to him. This is a bandage, he thought. It doesn't change their reality, deal with systemic problems of poverty, or even get them lunch tomorrow. And while I agree all those things need to be addressed by Christians and all people of good will—he's wrong that opening your soul to God in prayer is a bandage. It's a life source. It is a move that gives you energy to move through to the next day. It gives you hope, strength, a future, and it gives you love.

God loves you. But unless you do something that indicates an openness to God's love, a move to receiving it, you will not feel it. And when you do, you will be (as well as feel) fully alive—even if you are on your deathbed.

Dying Is Safe, And Spiritually Fruitful: The Mystery of Self-Gift

One of the things that makes us want to grip control in the face of dying is a primordial sense that dying is "not safe." And it is a natural, self-protective reaction: we avoid placing our hands on hot stoves; we don't step out on thin ice. Psychologists argue that, for healthy people, it takes enormous effort to overcome the natural resistance to killing oneself. In cases of physician-assisted suicide, when it is a deliberate choice, the driver to overcoming that natural resistance is fear.

But there is nothing to be afraid of when dying in Christ. Paul put it powerfully:

> But in fact Christ has been raised from the dead, the first fruits of those who have died. For since death came through a human being, the resurrection of the dead has also come through a human being; for as all die in Adam, so all will be made alive in Christ. But each in his own order: Christ the first fruits, then at his coming those who belong to Christ. (1 Cor 15:20–23)
>
> Listen, I will tell you a mystery! We will not all die, but we will all be changed, in a moment, in the twinkling of an eye, at the last trumpet. For the trumpet will sound, and the dead will be raised imperishable, and we will be changed. For this perishable body must put on imperishability, and this mortal body must put on immortality. When this perishable body puts on imperishability, and this mortal body puts on immortality, then the saying that is written will be fulfilled: "Death has been swallowed up in victory." "Where, O death, is your victory? Where, O death, is your sting?" The sting of death is sin, and the power of sin is the law. But thanks be to God,

who gives us the victory through our Lord Jesus Christ.
(1 Cor 15:51–27)

If we can understand—or if not understand, trust—that death is not the end of everything, but an offering of ourselves to God, then Paul's message resonates more powerfully.

> But someone will ask, "How are the dead raised? . . . What you sow does not come to life unless it dies. And as for what you sow, you do not sow the body that is to be, but a bare seed, perhaps of wheat or of some other grain. But God gives it a body as he has chosen, and to each kind of seed its own body. (1 Cor 15:25–38)

The strange, extraordinary, God-inflected truth is that dying in Christ is safe and spiritually fruitful. The act of dying well, offering one's life as seed to be sown, raises so much fruit: comfort to the family, reconciliation to loved ones, witness to the caregivers, opportunities to care and love, shared prayer and increased bonds of Christian brotherhood and sisterhood.

The mystery of self-gift is not simply offering yourself as a lamb to the slaughter—although there is plenty of mystery in the offering of the Lamb of God to his death on a cross. The mystery of self-gift is a handing over of one's life to the one who will nourish us through this narrow passage and into new life. In a way, it is like entrusting your journey to a guide. But it is more than that. It is offering your life in exchange for God's life.

Dying Has Been Shaped To Help You Prepare for the Great Exchange of Life: Your Life for God's Life

I want to underline one more time: dying is not sunshine and buttercups. It is not a grace in itself; it is the consequence of original sin. Humanity's sinful actions opened a space in God's good creation that resulted in death, a death that was not intended for us. God did not create death, and it shows. Illness and decay do not come from God. But God did shape death in a way that prepares us for more, infinitely more: your life opening to God and allowing him to lift you up and transform your life. Not because more life is good (although it is), but because life in relationship with Christ is the best, most beautiful thing we could ever hope for. We do not "become god" in this exchange, but in dying, God transforms us and lives in us in a way that makes us fully, gloriously alive.

Has God ever been the distant, original "clock-maker," as Deists would hold? The Spirit of God (Hebrew, *ruach*) is the breath of life: the Hebrew *ruach* means Spirit, breath, and wind. The universe breathes with the Spirit of God, and is sustained by this breath. Humanity was created through the breath of life (see Genesis: he blew into Adam the breath of life). When we reach the end of our days and draw our last breath, God is breathing with you—and when you stop breathing, his breath carries you into the next path. God's life and breath sustains you into the next life, until the resurrection of the body on the last day. It's not a simple exchange of life, but more a recognition that you have no life apart from the goodness and love of God. The more you give to him with an open heart, the more he offers. We cannot outdo God in generosity.

Much of this book has been written to encourage you to take dying as an opportunity to turn to God. Dying is tragic and not part of God's original plan, but God is bigger than any tragedy created by human hands. There is a way that when we reach the shore of our own existence, we may be more open to the shoreline of God's reality. God is always present, but our awareness of that presence is heightened. Our willingness to see is sharpened. Our openness to love is deepened. Our awareness of the spiritual in times of physical weakness to illumined.

Don't Take the Bait: Tricks of the Heart

This book began with a quotation from Jeremiah 9:17: "The heart is devious above all else; it is perverse—who can understand it?" This isn't meant to be especially bleak. It is meant to communicate that we are often confused about the things that matter most, colored by emotions, assumptions, and temptations. And when confronted with the brave new world of physician-assisted suicide and euthanasia, where relationships, fears, medicine, presumptions, loss, and hope collide, it is easy for the heart to be tricked.

But remember, Jeremiah is also the source of one of the most comforting pieces of Scripture in the whole Bible: "I know the plans I have for you, says the Lord; plans of fullness, not of harm; to give you a future and a hope." There is no asterisk on that statement that says ". . .unless you're dying." God has plans of fullness for you, not of harm. I encourage you to open yourself to God's life in every way possible, but start with one small step. With that small step, you offer your life to God in trust that he will nourish you into eternal life.

Don't let your heart be tricked. How do you give your dying body to God?

APPENDIX I

Letter to Ministers

How Do We Teach People To Die Well?

~

D ear ministers of all types,

If you have read through this book to its end, you may realize: we have a problem. The problem in this small book is presented in terms of a cultural decision point about physician-assisted suicide. The bigger problem is that most Americans, whether Christian or not, don't know how to die well—and have no idea where to start.

This is not the way Christianity used to be. The *ars moriendi* (art of dying) used to be the bread and butter of Christian pastoral practice. St. Robert Bellarmine's *The Art of Dying* was the equivalent of a best seller in the first days of the printing press. But soon after that came the Enlightenment, and the rise of modern medical science . . . in many ways, a very positive development, but one that increasingly separated out the spiritual dimension of dying from the physical. Additionally, all attention began to be placed on modern medicine's promise of a cure. As I mentioned in chapter 1, this evolved into a cultural understanding of death that met dying as failure, as unexpected, and as best handled by medical professionals. Although we still have some distinctive rituals around dying (especially in Catholicism, around the anointing of the sick), this is a far cry from the deliberate attention paid in centuries past—a process that began with the inception of the illness, and was recognized as ritual, as normative, as a teaching moment, and as an unavoidable but accepted part of the Christian life.

When I was initially doing research on how people die in contemporary church life, I asked a good number of priests if they were ever trained to teach people how to die, if they actually do teach people how to die. I was met with many stricken, deer-in-the-headlights looks. Some offered that they got a taste of this in CPE (Clinical Pastoral Education, a nationwide program)—but only a taste, as CPE tended to be oriented toward dying as crisis and last moments. If we need to teach people how to die, it needs to be before they reach their final days.

It's no wonder that, in this vacuum, people are turning to creating their own rituals—including physician-assisted suicide.

So what can we do?

1. Teaching how to die well is, paradoxically, teaching how to live well.[1] Living with courage. Living with honesty. Acknowledging emotions. Saying I'm sorry. Being merciful to others. Asking for help. Saying I love you. Looking at life within an eternal horizon. These are not realities foreign to the Christian life. Helping people die well involves reminding them what has (hopefully) been a story throughout their lives . . . and if it hasn't, it's never too late to change the direction of the story.

---

1. I am not the first to note this disconnection between medicine and theology in the art of dying well, and others have written suggestive books that do focus on how to reconnect the two and focus on living well through and beyond dying. Some books I recommend: Swinton and Payne, eds., *Living Well and Dying Gracefully*; Vogt, *Patience, Compassion, Hope, and the Christian Art of Dying Well*; Craddock, Goldsmith, and Goldsmith, *Speaking of Dying*; and Moll, *The Art of Dying*.

2. One problem, however, is that when pastors and ministers are engaged, it is at the end of the dying process. In fact, people often don't know that they are dying until the end . . . they know they are fighting a serious disease, but it is unclear whether it will end in their death. People facing serious illness need a lever they can pull that indicates to the church that they are seriously ill. I make humble suggestions below.

   a. Chaplains in hospital or hospice settings do a lot of this work. But perhaps we need to do outreach through churches and charitable organizations, because people first discover their critical illness outside of hospital stays and hospices. Create an apostolate or outreach to provide spiritual support to those living with illness. Advertise. Make a big announcement of it within churches, and encourage people to bring anyone who needs this kind of connection and help. I can imagine this as a stand-alone ministry supported by multiple churches, or as work supported by Catholic Charities (or another faith-affiliated charitable organization). While you can encourage doctors to make referrals, I personally think it best to create this initiative outside the hospital and hospice walls, in a collaborative but not dependent relationship.

   b. Educate those who are already meeting people living with critical illness. Befrienders ministry is a popular ministry to the home bound (and while the home bound are not necessarily the critically ill, there is overlap). Many churches have lay people deliver communion to shut-ins. How can we deepen those ministries—or train the volunteers in them to recognize when to make a referral?

   c. For many years, we have heard that more people want spiritual direction than there are spiritual directors. If there is ever a time for a person so inclined to engage in spiritual direction, it is at a time of critical illness. The need is clear. While not everyone is called to be a spiritual director, many are. We need to find a way to meet the need for spiritual direction in his population with the call many have received to offer spiritual direction. If the church is first about salvation of souls, this would seem to be a no-brainer. But how and where this would be offered and where this would be housed is a tricky question.

d. Recover Christian ritual. People need ritual, and if they don't inherit it, they will create it. Recover and re-present the rituals of dying from the ages. People often say "I don't know what to do" in situations like this. Do ritual: the rosary, the chaplet of divine mercy, liturgy of the hours, repeating "life verses" from Scripture, etc.

3. One of the reasons I wrote this book was to challenge the rising cultural narrative on physician-assisted suicide. We need to challenge these "tricks of the heart" because they are wrong in ways people only come to realize as the implications are unpacked. But this is a book playing defense. If you are counseling someone, look for the root of these tricks: fear, control, depression. The best defense is not purely reactive, but finds the cause of the offensive move and addresses it.

But we also need a strong offense. That is, *be an apostle of hope*. Carry the hope of Jesus Christ to that person. Remember that an encounter with God is the best (and sometimes only) way that living with dying makes sense.

This can be hard, because it is relatively easy to meet someone in their pain, to empathize—at least by comparison. Indeed, never approach a person in critical illness without compassion. If you cannot do that, you need to go home. But it is harder to bring all three of the theological virtues—love, *and* faith, *and* hope—to a vulnerable person being tempted by tricks.

There is no technique to being an apostle of hope, but I have suspicions as to how these people are formed.

1. Pay attention to your own formation and prayer life. You cannot give what you do not have. Bearing peace is the strongest sign of hope in situations like these.

2. If you feel especially weak or wounded, point in faith to the One who heals all weakness and woundedness. This is not about you, after all. You can be wounded and still point the way in faith.

3. Remember that your weakness is a place for God to break in . . . in your own life, and through you to others. Sometimes (especially in hard conversations) I ask God to let me be a sieve for the Holy Spirit. I pray to "get out of the way" of God's work. But paradoxically, that means that I humbly must be present.

4. Offer to pray with that person. (Not just for, but with.) He or she may not have the words. You will. Even something as simple as a prayerful Our Father strengthens, shares, and points in the right direction.

5. There are many scriptural quotations that shimmer with hope. Write them down. Offer them. Leave them with the person. If I had to choose three, they would be these:

> Blessed be the God and Father of our Lord Jesus Christ! By his great mercy he has given us a new birth into a living hope through the resurrection of Jesus Christ from the dead, and into an inheritance that is imperishable, undefiled, and unfading, kept in heaven for you, who are being protected by the power of God through faith for a salvation ready to be revealed in the last time.
>
> In this you rejoice, even if now for a little while you have had to suffer various trials, so that the genuineness of your faith—being more precious than gold that, though perishable, is tested by fire—may be found to result in praise and glory and honor when Jesus Christ is revealed. Although you have not seen him, you love him; and even though you do not see him now, you believe in him and rejoice with an indescribable and glorious joy,

for you are receiving the outcome of your faith, the salvation of your souls. (1 Peter 3–9)

and

For surely I know the plans I have for you, says the Lord, plans for your welfare and not for harm, to give you a future with hope (Jer 29:11).

and

The Lord, your God, is in your midst, a warrior who gives victory; he will rejoice over you with gladness, he will renew you in his love; he will exult over you with loud singing . . . (Zeph 3:17).

APPENDIX II

Letter to Family and Friends
How Do We Help Our Loved Ones Die?

~

Dear friends in caregiving and in Christ,

First, I am sorry. Helping someone you love die, while experiencing your own grief and (often) managing his or her health care is emotionally tiring and difficult.

Second, you may want to read the appendix letter directed to ministers . . . because while that section was directed toward ecclesial ministers, you are "ministering" to your loved one through your everyday presence. Your work here is incredibly significant.

But this could be another book. What I present here will be brief and, hopefully, suggestive. When it comes right down to it, there is no lock-step "right way" to help someone die well. But there are patterns in a good death.

First: remember that in many ways, nothing has changed. You are still that person's spouse, or friend, or adult child. You may be taking on greater responsibilities for the one who is dying, but you are still in the same relationship. Find ways to love the person. Affection, concern, and (when appropriate) light-hearted conversation go a long way. So many people I have met living with critical illness wanted so much to be treated as they were before: a person with particular relationships, interests, and habits. Sometimes love and friendship is as simple as that—enjoying each other and living out your relationships. But don't shy away from the "big" conversations when your loved one is initiating them.

Second: accept help in your caregiving. People are probably asking what they can do to help. But it can be easier to do things yourself than accept a one-time offer, right? Yet there are things that can be done. If you are at home, have a list by your door of what can be done quickly—give people a choice! Wash dishes, clean the bathroom, do the laundry and bring it back folded, a list of recipes or meals that you and your family can eat, a shopping list, mow the lawn. If they can stay with your loved one, go take a walk or go to church or take a nap, whatever you need. Or simply visit with your friend.

Or perhaps your loved one who is dying does not want anyone but you around. That is a hard situation, but you need to convince him or her that you will be better able to take care of him or her if you can connect with others or get some fresh air (I am talking about a daily break, not an extended vacation, of course). Get his or her doctor to back you on this.

Third: offer to pray with your loved one. This may be extremely uncomfortable if you have no habit of this. But there is no time like the present. Don't assume he or she won't want to; you may be surprised. All you have to do is offer to pray a known prayer (say, the Our Father) with him or her, and more if you are inspired. If he or she is in a coma, singing a hymn to him or her may be welcome. If he/she says no, go ahead and pray anyway (but when your loved one is resting or sleeping).

Pray for what? It may have been a while for you, too—or perhaps not, but given the circumstances, you may not know where to start. Pray for what you want. It can be as simple as that, and it is honest. But you can also add to that: Lord, pour yourself into this person. Give her what she most truly needs. Give me what I most truly need. Only you know what that is. Grant us peace.

Ritual prayers can help. If you are Catholic, praying the rosary is a time-honored tradition. If you are unfamiliar with the prayers, you can find it online and pray along.

Fourth: offer to connect this person with a chaplain, a priest, or a minister. If he/she says no, that is their right, but you may want to gently ask—why not? The reasons could be fairly specious and easily resolved. Or perhaps you'll get a response like "I'm not that close to dying yet!"—at which point you can assure the person that a visit for spiritual support doesn't mean you are dying within hours or even days or weeks. If you are Catholic, a person with a grave illness who requests sacramental anointing can receive it at any time, and given that it is a gift from God that strengthens the person, if should be received sooner rather than later. But if your loved one doesn't want to meet with a chaplain or priest, perhaps you should anyway. You need spiritual support right now as well. And remember that people's minds can change—leave the offer to contact a priest open, if you can.

Fifth: Remember God, and let go. Much of this book tries to convince the one who is facing death to give him or herself to God, that death can help ready a person for God's embrace and homecoming. Loving without clinging is your difficult task. Support him or her, but when the time comes, entrust him or her to God's hands. It is wisdom and no shame to ask God for help in doing this.

If they say they want to die, don't assume that means they want assisted suicide. It easily could mean they want to hurt less, to stop saying goodbye, to stop living in the twilight zone. It could mean they are frustrated or depressed or angry. Try to help them target the real issue behind the statement, and try to help them address that. You may not be able to "make it better." But perhaps your concern and listening and attempt to lend a hand will help them realize they are supported.

If they do say they want to end their own life, I will be blunt: do not agree to it. The best hope you have for them changing their mind is not agreeing to it. You can say, look, you are still alive and I love you, and will stay with you every step of the way. But I can't be a part of this. God does not want you to do this. God has a plan that is better than assisted suicide. You can't prevent them from following through, but you can make clear you think it is a horrible mistake.

As I was finishing this book, a friend and theologian, Janet Smith, had just buried her mother after years of direct caregiving. I will end with her words:

> Thinking about the last weeks and days of my mother's life and of a friend whose father is likely dying. She doesn't want to see him suffer; she doesn't want to let him go. The wisdom of leaving death in God's hands is so right. If we were to be the ones who decide, we would likely do one of two things, both wrong. For those who suffer and whose lives seem without value to them or others, we would likely kill them out of a sense of mercy. There would also be those who would keep their loved ones alive way past when their "time had come" if they could, just to have one more day, hour, minute to hold their hands or caress their brow. God has reserved the time of death for Himself and that is so clearly right to me now, experientially so as well as logically so.
>
> Moreover, it is also experientially clear to me now that deep within the person who seems to be nearly a "mere vegetable" there may well be powerful things going on—sorting things out, talking with God. It is best for us not to disturb or short circuit that process. I think all the hymns I sang and prayers I said aloud and my talking to my mother about Jesus (she wanted me to talk with her about Jesus when she could indicate her desires—I wish I had done more of that)—and of heaven, were very valuable and blessed moments. I believe they helped her "transition."[2]

May our Lord grant us all the grace of a peaceful transition from this life to the next.

---

2. Smith, social media post, October 2016.

Bibliography

Ariès, Philippe. *The Hour of our Death*. Translated by Helen Weaver. New York: Oxford University Press, 1991.

Beilock, Sian. *How the Body Knows Its Mind: The Surprising Power of the Physical Environment to Influence How You Think and Feel*. New York: Atria, 2015.

Bellarmino, Roberto Francesco Romolo, and John Dalton. *The Art of Dying Well, (or, How to Be a Saint, Now and Forever)*. Manchester, NH: Sophia Institute, 2005.

Benedict XVI. *Spe Salvi*. The Vatican, November 30, 2007. http://w2.vatican.va/content/benedict-xvi/en/encyclicals/documents/hf_ben-xvi_enc_20071130_spe-salvi.html.

Buchbinder, Justin. "Cultural Traditions and Respect for Elders." *Strength for Caring: Respect for Caregivers*, accessed Feb 1, 2013. http://www.strengthforcaring.com/manual/about-you-celebrating-cultures/cultural-traditions-and-respect-for-elders.

Callahan, Daniel. *The Troubled Dream of Life: In Search of a Peaceful Death*. Washington, DC: Georgetown University Press, 2000.

Callanan, Maggie, and Patricia Kelley. *Final Gifts: Understanding the Special Awareness, Needs, and Communications of the Dying*. New York: Poseidon, 1992.

Cameli, Louis J. *The Devil You Don't Know: Recognizing and Resisting Evil in Everyday Life*. Notre Dame, IN: Ave Maria, 2011.

Catechism of the Catholic Church. Vatican City: Libreria Editrice Vaticana. Washington, DC: Distributed by United States Catholic Conference, 2000.

Craddock, Fred B., Dale Goldsmith, and Joy V. Goldsmith. *Speaking of Dying: Recovering the Church's Voice in the Face of Death*. Grand Rapids: Brazos, 2012.

Doerflinger, Richard, and Carlos Gomez. "Killing the Pain, Not the Patient: Palliative Care vs Assisted Suicide." United States Conference of Catholic

Bishops, accessed May 19, 2016. http://www.usccb.org/about/pro-life-activities/respect-life-program/killing-the-pain.cfm.

Eastwood, Clint, et al. *Million Dollar Baby*. Burbank, CA: Warner Home Video, 2005.

"End of Life: Helping with Comfort and Care." National Institute on Aging, accessed November 9, 2016. https://www.nia.nih.gov/health/publication/end-life-helping-comfort-and-care/providing-comfort-end-life.

de Caussade, Jean Pierre. *Abandonment to Divine Providence*. New York: Image, 1975.

"Disability Groups Opposed to Assisted Suicide Laws." *Not Dead Yet*. Accessed November 7, 2016. http://notdeadyet.org/disability-groups-opposed-to-assisted-suicide-laws.

Ely, E. Wesley. "Sonnet XXX: Love, Dignity, and Dying." *The Linacre Quarterly*. 83, no. 2 (2016) 150–56.

Glatzer, Richard, et al. *Still Alice*. Sony Pictures Home Entertainment, 2015.

Hendin, Herbert, and Kathleen Foley. "Physician-Assisted Suicide in Oregon: A Medical Perspective." *Michigan Law Review*. 106, no. 8 (2008) 1613–39.

Indelicato, Rose Anne. "The Advanced Practice Nurse's Role in Palliative Care and the Management of Dyspnea." *Topics in Advanced Practice Nursing eJournal* 6, no. 4 (2006): http://www.medscape.com/viewarticle/551364_7.

Ignatius of Antioch. "Ignatius to the Ephesians." *Early Christian Writings*. Accessed November 15, 2016. http://www.earlychristianwritings.com/text/ignatius-ephesians-lightfoot.html.

John Paul II. *Crossing the Threshold of Hope*. Edited by Vittorio Messori. London: Jonathan Cape, 1994.

Jones, David Albert. "Assisted Suicide and Euthanasia: A Guide to the Evidence." *Anscombe Bioethics Centre*, Oxford University. August 10, 2015. http://www.bioethics.org.uk/evidenceguide.pdf.

"Josephine Bakhita." *Catholic Online*. Accessed January 19, 2017. http://www.catholic.org/saints/saint.php?saint_id=5601.

"Josephine Bakhita." *The Vatican*. Accessed January 19, 2017. http://www.vatican.va/news_services/liturgy/saints/ns_lit_doc_20001001_giuseppina-bakhita_en.html.

Kavanaugh, John F. *Who Count As Persons?: Human Identity and the Ethics of Killing*. Washington, DC: Georgetown University Press, 2001.

Kübler-Ross, Elisabeth. *On Death and Dying*. New York: Macmillan, 1969.

Lamott, Anne. *Grace (Eventually): Thoughts on Faith*. New York: Riverhead, 2007.

———. *Traveling Mercies: Some Thoughts on Faith*. New York: Anchor, 2000.

Lewis, C. S. *The Lion, the Witch, and the Wardrobe*. New York: HarperCollins, 1994.

———. *The Problem of Pain*. New York: HarperOne, 2001.

Lipka, Michael. "Why America's 'Nones' Left Religion Behind." *Fact Tank: News in the Numbers* (blog), The Pew Research Center, August 26, 2016. http://

Bibliography

www.pewresearch.org/fact-tank/2016/08/24/why-americas-nones-left-religion-behind/.

Lowry, Lois. *The Giver*. New York: Houghton Mifflin Harcourt, 1993.

Maclean, Norman. *A River Runs Through It, and Other Stories*. New York: Pocket, 1992.

Marcel, Gabriel. *Being and Having: An Existentialist Diary*. New York: Harper & Row, 1965.

McGill, Arthur Chute. *Death and Life: An American Theology*. Edited by Charles A. Wilson and Per M. Anderson. Eugene, OR: Wipf and Stock, 2003.

McPherson, Christine J., Keith G. Wilson, Michelle M. Lobchuk, and Susan Brajtman. "Family Caregivers' Assessment of Symptoms in Patients with Advanced Cancer: Concordance with Patients and Factors Affecting Accuracy." *Journal of Pain and Symptom Management*. 35, no. 1 (2008) 70–82.

Moll, Rob. *The Art of Dying: Living Fully into the Life to Come*. Downers Grove, IL: InterVarsity, 2010.

Mueller, Lisel. *Alive Together: New and Selected Poems*. Baton Rouge, LA: Louisiana State University Press, 1996.

Murphy, Beverly Bigtree. *he used to be Somebody: A Journey into Alzheimer's Disease Through the Eyes of a Caregiver*. Boulder, CO: Gibbs Associates, 1995.

Nichols, Terence L. *Death and Afterlife: A Theological Introduction*. Grand Rapids: Brazos, 2010.

"NHPCO Facts and Figures report, Hospice Care in America: 2012," Annual overview, National Hospice and Palliative Care Organization, 2012. http://www.nhpco.org/sites/default/files/public/Statistics_Research/2012_Facts_Figures.pdf.

"Oregon's Death With Dignity Act—2014." Evaluation research, Oregon Public Health Division, 2014. https://public.health.oregon.gov/Provider PartnerResources/EvaluationResearch/DeathwithDignityAct/Documents /year17.pdf.

"Paying for Hospice: Medicare / Medicaid / More Options." Web page, Hospice Directory, accessed November 1, 2016. http://www.hospicedirectory.org/cm/about/paying.

Redford, Robert, dir. *A River Runs Through It*. Starring Craig Sheffer, Brad Pitt, Tom Skerritt, Brenda Blethyn, and Emily Lloyd. Based on *A River Runs Through It* by Norman Maclean. Burbank, CA: Columbia TriStar Home Video, 1999.

Rosenblatt, Roger. "The Disease That Takes Your Breath Away." *Time*, April 30, 2001. http://content.time.com/time/magazine/article/0,9171,999776,00.html.

Ruffing, Janet. *Spiritual Direction: Beyond the Beginnings*. New York: Paulist, 2000.

Ryan, Barbara Shlemon. *Healing Prayer*. Notre Dame, IN: Ave Maria, 1976.

Sanford, Agnes Mary White. *The Healing Light*. New York: Ballantine, 1983.

Sontag, Susan. *Illness As Metaphor; and, AIDS and Its Metaphors.* New York: Doubleday, 1990.

"Statistics." *National Institute of Mental Health.* Accessed December 1, 2016. https://www.nimh.nih.gov/health/statistics/index.shtml.

Stoddard, Sandol. *The Hospice Movement: A Better Way of Caring for the Dying.* New York: Vintage, 1992.

Swinton, John, and Richard Payne, eds. *Living Well and Dying Faithfully: Christian Practices for End-of-Life Care.* Grand Rapids: Eerdmans, 2009.

Thienpont, L., M. Verhofstadt, T. Van Loon, et al. "Euthanasia Requests, Procedures and Outcomes for 100 Belgian Patients Suffering from Psychiatric Disorders: A Retrospective, Descriptive Study." *BMJ Open* 5 (2015): e007454, doi: 10.1136/bmjopen-2014-007454.

Verghese, Abraham. *My Own Country: A Doctor's Story.* New York: Vintage, 1995.

Vogt, Christopher P. *Patience, Compassion, Hope, and the Christian Art of Dying Well.* Lanham, MD: Rowman & Littlefield, 2004.

Wink, Walter. *Engaging the Powers: Discernment and Resistance in a World of Domination.* Minneapolis: Fortress, 1992.

Subject Index

Subject Index

Hauerwas, Stanley, 38–39
Holy Spirit, the, xvi, 15, 50–51, 63, 67, 74, 83–84, 88, 99
hope, xi-xii, 29, 36, 44, 49, 59, 62–67, 70, 73–74, 76, 84, 89, 92–93, 96, 98–100, 103
hospice, xiv, xv, 18–21, 26, 28, 40, 41, 46, 48, 54, 86, 97
human dignity, 45–46, 51, 56

Irenaeus of Lyons, 88

Job (Biblical figure), 22
John Paul II, 60

Kübler-Ross, Elisabeth, 68

Lewis, C.S., 22, 79
Lamott, Anne, 41–44

Marcel, Gabriel, 7–10
McGill, Arthur C., 22–24
medicinal shaping of death, the, 57–59
mental illness, 47, 68–72, 75
Million Dollar Baby, 10–12
Mueller, Lisel, 62–63

nephesh, 3
Not Dead Yet (disability advocacy group), 5

original sin, 3–4, 5, 22, 51, 55, 57–58, 78, 91

palliative care, xii, 16–21, 84, 87
pouring (scriptural metaphor), 81–83

protection, xv, 11–13, 54–58, 86, 90, 99

reconciliation (between persons), 26–27, 91
reconciliation (with God), 15, 27–28, 86
resistance (in spiritual direction), 25
Rosenblatt, Roger, 39

sacramental anointing, 27, 80–84, 96, 103
Saunders, Cicely, 22
Shlemon, Barbara, 27–28
Sontag, Susan, 39
soul, 2–4, 8, 10, 15, 33, 50–51, 75, 81, 89, 98, 100
spiritual direction, 25, 97–98
Still Alice (movie), 39
suicide, Catholic Church position, 75–76
suffering, definition, 31
suffering, meaning of, 31–35
suffering, offering to God, 32–35

"technological brinkmanship," xiv
Temple of the Holy Spirit, the, 15
"terror disease," 39
The Art of Dying (book), 95
theodicy, 22

unity of body and soul, 3–4

Verghese, Abraham, xvi
vulnerability, human, 9, 13, 29–30, 56, 79

weakness, fear of, 13–15